George Rundle Prynne

The Soldier's Dying Vision

And other Poems and Hymns

George Rundle Prynne

The Soldier's Dying Vision
And other Poems and Hymns

ISBN/EAN: 9783337307059

Printed in Europe, USA, Canada, Australia, Japan

Cover: Foto ©Thomas Meinert / pixelio.de

More available books at **www.hansebooks.com**

THE

SOLDIER'S DYING VISIONS;

AND

Other Poems and Hymns.

BY

GEORGE RUNDLE PRYNNE, *M.A.*,

VICAR OF S. PETER'S, PLYMOUTH.

LONDON ·
J. MASTERS AND CO., 78, NEW BOND STREET.
MDCCCLXXXI.

To

MY DEAR CHILDREN

I DEDICATE THESE PAGES,

As a Memento

IN DAYS TO COME

OF HAPPY DAYS GONE BY,

IN THE OLD HOME.

A 2

PREFACE.

THE Poems and Hymns contained in this volume were written in fragments of time during five-and-twenty years of a busy life. The first three were read at Social Parochial Entertainments. Perhaps I may be presumptuous in hoping that a larger public will to some extent endorse the approval which they received in a more limited and indulgent circle. Some of the hymns have already appeared in various Hymn Books for public worship, and one little hymn has found its way into most English Hymnals. I have always readily acceded to the request for their being thus used, and esteem it a privilege that anything I have written should be thought suitable for so high and sacred a purpose.

G. R. P.

CONTENTS.

Contents

Christian Soldier's Dying Visions.

T HE visions of my troubled life
Are floating through my brain ;
My boyhood and my manhood's days
I seem to live again.

I see the dear old cottage home
Close by the sheltering wood,
The flowers, the walk, the garden-gate,
Just as of old they stood.

I see the village church hard by,
I hear the bells so sweet
Calling us forth each Sunday morn
Our risen Lord to greet.

B

The worthy priest is speaking now—
How well I know that voice—
Entreating me in early youth
To make the Lord my choice;

To shun the wide well-trodden road,
And choose the narrow way
Leading through earthly toil and care
To heaven's eternal day.

'Tis evening now; around the fire,
With sisters sitting nigh,
I catch that glimpse of heaven below—
My mother's loving eye.

'Tis fixed on me, as if to pierce,
With love's keen vision bright,
The clouds which hide my future life
From its far-reaching sight.

O vision bright of peace and love,
My childhood's happy home!
Symbol of that still deeper peace
Which soon, I trust, will come.

And now again I hear the call
  Which fired my youthful heart,
To quit my home, and in the strife
  Of men tó take my part.

I feel again upon my breast
  My mother's fond embrace ;
I see the sparkling tears of love
  Upon each sister's face.

I tear myself from these to seek
  For glory and renown ;
I spurn the rustic's quiet life
  To win the victor's crown.

And now I hear the battle's roar,
  I join the deadly strife,
Where men with men are struggling
  For victory and life.

I hear the rattling musketry,
  I hear the cannon's boom,
Bringing to comrades all around
  The message of their doom.

I hear the shouts of triumph now,
　　I hear the cries of pain ;
'Tis passing all in memory
　　Before my soul again.

The cavalry are charging now ;
　　" Form quickly into square."
They stop, they waver, they retreat
　　With many a saddle bare.

But oh, it was a saddening sight
　　To see those gallant men
Falling beneath our withering fire,
　　Never to rise again !

Their faces often haunt me still ;
　　They are before me now,
Courage and resolution stamped
　　On every manly brow.

I have no time to think ; arise,
　　Form quickly into line,
The enemy are flying ! charge,
　　Double up the incline !

Onward we rush, half wild with joy,
    Yet steady as a rock.
We reach the height, our foes are gone,
    They could not stand our shock.

My GOD, my GOD, forgive me now
    If, midst the deadly din,
My passions got the mastery,
    And led me into sin.

My GOD, my GOD, forgive me now,
    If thoughts of earthly fame
Fired my heart with eagerness
    To make myself a name.

Ah ! what is now the maddening sound
    Which breaks upon my ear?
It is the shout of victory,
    The thrilling British cheer.

It makes my very heart's blood run
    Tingling through every vein ;
E'en now, the memory of that shout
    Warms my old blood again.

Oh, who can tell the throbs of joy
Which fill the soldier's heart,
When victory has crowned the fight
In which he took his part !

Yet now I do remember well,
Amidst the anthem's strain,
Which told that England's gallant sons
Had fought and won again,—

The vision of my mother's love,
My sister's last farewell,
Like lightning flashed across my soul,
Midst all the triumph swell.

What will our people think at home ?
What will my mother say ?
What will my loving sisters feel
When *they* hear of this day ?

This day of triumph to our arms,
In which I did my part ;
What will they think, and feel, and say ?
Oh, how this thrilled my heart !

Aye, more than all the shouts of joy
    Which fire the soldier's breast,
When he his duty well has done,
    And God has done the rest.

My GOD, I did not Thee forget
    Midst all that deadly strife ;
I asked for victory, I asked
    For pardon, and for life.

And Thou didst grant my prayer, O GOD,
    Thanks to Thy holy name ;
Thou didst grant more, Thy saving grace,
    Better than earthly fame,—

Thy saving grace, to give to Thee
    The remnant of my days,
And learn to live and trust Thee well,
    And walk in Thy blest ways.

Two contests have been mine throughout
    The time here granted me—
One for my Queen and country, one,
    My heavenly King, for Thee.

And now my end is drawing near,
My fighting days are past,
One battle only now remains,
My greatest and my last.

Jesus, true Captain of my soul,
In this my final strife,
Oh, grant me victory in death,
And then eternal life !

My prayer is heard ; I hear His voice
Calling His soldier home ;
I go from glories that have passed
To glories yet to come.

Telemachus.

THE weak Honorius had, on the occasion of his sixth consulate, restored to life an entirely pagan institution—the celebration of the secular games, and had specially included in it the combats of gladiators. When the announcement of these games had been published everywhere in all the empire, and had thus penetrated into the deserts, a monk, until then unknown, named Telemachus, of Nitria according to some, of Phrygia according to others, took one of those resolutions, the simple grandeur and immense results of which appear only after their accomplishment. He left his cell, travelled from the depths of the east to Rome, arrived there in time to be present at the imperial solemnities, entered the Colosseum, burst through the waves of people all palpitating with a ferocious curiosity, and threw himself between the gladiators engaged in combat. The indignant spectators pursued this untimely interrupter, this fool, this black fanatic, first with ferocious clamours, then with blows of stones and sticks. Stoned like the first martyr of Christianity, Telemachus fell, and the gladiators whom he had desired to separate completed the work. But his blood was the last shed in that arena where so much blood had flowed. The nobleness of his sacrifice showed the full horror of the abuse which he would have overthrown. An edict of Honorius

proscribed for ever the games of the gladiators. From
that day they are no more heard of in history. The crime
of so many centuries was extinguished by the blood of a
monk, who happened to be a hero.*

MONTALEMBERT'S *Monks of the West.*

STERN resolution stamped upon his brow,
Telemachus forsakes his desert home ;
Sadly and patiently he treads the way
Towards the vast city, old Imperial Rome.

Long has he dwelt in Nitria's desert wild,
Shunning the false ways of this sinful earth ;
Striving, by vigil, fast, and fervent prayer,
Worthy to live of his celestial birth.

What urges thee, O saintly man of GOD,
Again to seek the world thou once didst shun ?
Has Rome no dangers now for faithful souls,
Who in their Christian course would safely run ?

---

* The incident of the death of Telemachus in the Colosseum
is recorded by Theodoret and Cassiodorus. (Theod., *Hist. Eccles.*,
cap. xxiv., lib. 5 ; Cassiod., ix., c. iii. ; see *Roba di Roma*,
vol. i., p. 233.)

Dost thou repent the step thou once didst take,
When thou didst leave the world, at JESUS' call,
Counting things earthly but as worthless dust,
If thou couldst JESUS gain—Thy LORD, Thy ALL?

Oh no, vain pleasures cannot lure thee forth
From the true pleasures which have long been thine;
False lights of earth cannot again bedaze
The soul which long has lived in light divine.

Yet the monk presses on with eager steps,
Resting but little on his dreary way;
Braving alike the perils of the night,
And the fierce burning of the noontide day.

And now, his journey o'er, the saintly monk
Reaches the city he has sought so long;
Weary and faint he treads the crowded streets,
And hears again Rome's revelry and song.

CHORUS.

To-morrow, brave Romans,
The games will begin;
And noble Honorius
Will usher them in.

The old Colosseum
Again will resound
With thousands of voices,
All crowded around.

Well-trained gladiators,
In close deadly strife,
Will fight, as men will fight,
For death or for life.
And lions and tigers,
From many a land,
Will stain with their life-blood
The dry, thirsty sand.   ·

Throughout all the empire
It has been made known,
That in all their glory
And ancient renown
The old Roman customs,
To all Romans dear,
In the old Colosseum
Again shall appear.

Telemachus.

The Christians may tell us
These games are all wrong,
But old Roman feeling
For them is too strong,
And though brave Honorius
Is Christian they say,
He gives the old Romans
Their loved holiday.

Then drink to the emperor :
Long may he reign,
To give us our old shows
Again and again.
As long as the old
Colosseum shall last,
May brave gladiators fight
As in the past.

My GOD, my GOD, forgive them ; they know not
Thee and Thy love, in JESUS CHRIST made known.
Oh, draw their hearts from these vile, sinful sights,
And make them worship Thee, and Thee alone.

Oh, give me wisdom, give me strength and grace,
Bravely and wisely to fulfil the part
Which, in Thy loving and mysterious ways,
I trust Thou hast implanted in my heart.

Thou knowest my unworthiness, O GOD,
Thou knowest also how my soul within,
Burns with an ardour I cannot resist,
To stop this devil's show, this deadly sin.

My GOD, protect me through the coming night;
Under me spread Thine everlasting arm.
Weary and faint I am, but Thou art strong.
Oh, grant me rest, and shield my soul from harm.

And when the morning dawns, oh, still be nigh
To fill my soul with grace and strength divine,
Calmly to meet the trials of the day,
And bring to good effect my heart's design.

Sweetly they rest, O GOD, who rest in Thee,
Sweeter than infant clasped to mother's breast;
Body and soul alike to Thee resigned,
Symbol on earth of Heaven's eternal rest.

Thus gavest Thou to Thy belovèd sleep ;
Thus slept Telemachus throughout the night
Before the day, which ushered in with pomp
The Roman games and gladiatorial fight.

In splendour rose the sun on ancient Rome,
Lighting up all the scene with southern glow,
As thousands went betimes places to gain,
Again to see old Rome's barbaric show.

The Colosseum in its glory stood,
Prepared to seat its thousands row by row ;
The coloured covering * all duly spread,
To shelter gazers from the sun's fierce glow.

Now shouts from twice ten thousand voices tell
That the great emperor is drawing nigh.
Hail, Cæsar, hail ! resounds from tier to tier,
As all take up the joyous, welcome cry.

The gladiators hear that thrilling shout
With hearts unshrinking, but with quickened breath ;

---

* In order to shelter people from the rays of the sun, it was
usual to spread an awning (*vela*) of white or coloured canvass
over the whole of the interior.

They know it is the prelude to a sign
Which calls them forth to victory or death.

Round the arena now, with heads erect
And measured tread, they walk in order meet,
Pausing but once their due salute to make
Before the mighty Cæsar's chosen seat.*

Hail, noble Cæsar! those about to die
Salute thee as they pass on to the fight;
Reign on in happiness o'er ancient Rome,
In all thy glory, majesty, and might.

And now they stand in all their manliness,
Conscious of strength and skill, a proud array,
Eager to win the victor's meed of praise,
Or die to make a Roman holiday.

The editor † selects two chosen men,
Who have the honour to begin the fray,
Which is to saturate with human blood
The dry arena on this festal day.

---

* The gladiators marched in procession into the arena,
saluting the emperor, if present, as they passed his seat.

† The person who presided over the exhibition was called the
editor.

The multitude with eagerness look on,
Watching the combatants with bated breath ;
For well 'tis known these gladiators brave
Intend to fight their combat unto death.

The well-trained men scan well each other's eyes,
Their short bright swords are flashing in the light,
Each tries to see some error in his foe,
Which may give him advantage in the fight.

On the bright helmet now a blow resounds,
Heard all the amphitheatre around,
For keen excitement holds the crowd in thrall,
As with strained nerves they watch for every sound.

But who is this thus madly rushing in,
Breaking through barriers, bounding o'er the sand,
Placing himself between the combatants,
Raising on high his supplicating hands?

"Stop ! stop ! I pray you, brave mistaken men,
I bid you stop in Christ's, my Master's, name ;
'Tis deadly sin for brothers thus to fight,
For Christians 'tis not glory, but foul shame.

C

"Stop! stop! I pray you, JESUS gives me strength
Thus to arrest you in your cruel fight;
Oh, think not of the plaudits of this crowd,
But what is just and holy in His sight!"

Thus spake the bold intruder as he stood
Watching the men with keen imploring eye;
No sign of fear was on his manly face,
He came prepared to suffer or to die.

The gladiators gazed on him with scorn,
Then raised their eyes towards the assembled crowd,
Who gave full vent to their excited wrath,
In shouts and execrations long and loud.

"Strike down the intruding monk," they hoarsely cry,
"The black fanatic who presumes to stay
The games fixed by the emperor's decree
To be enacted on this festive day!

"Beat him to death with sticks, or staves, or stones,
Crush him without a moment's more delay;
Let the attendants come with iron hooks,
And drag his worthless body fast away!"

All is confusion now in that vast throng,
So lately hushed in quietude profound;
Many leap o'er the barriers, and rush on
To dash the rash intruder to the ground.

Calmly Telemachus awaits his death,
For well he knows the meaning of this cry;
His body sinks upon the sandy plain,
His soul is raised to JESUS CHRIST on high.

The stones fall thickly on his noble brow,
His great heart still is fixed on CHRIST in Heaven;
He thinks not of himself, his last strong prayer
Is that his murderers may be forgiven.

A smile plays on the martyr's saintly face,
A vision bright sweetens his dying pain;
JESUS he feels accepts his sacrifice,
And tells him that his death is not in vain.

The gladiators close the dying scene,
Plunging their swords into his bruisèd breast;
The soul of brave Telemachus springs forth,
To enter on its everlasting rest.

Yet as his corse lay there, bleeding and torn,
Remorse and sorrow touched the Cæsar's heart;
He knew 'twas his decree that fixed these games,
He therefore in this murder had a part.

The dying martyr's vision is fulfilled,
Grace to the Emperor is given to say,
That human victims never more shall die
Merely to make a Roman holiday.

And never more in ancient Rome was known
The cruel sports held in the days gone by;
The hero monk, by his self-sacrifice,
Gained this great gift from his dear Lord on high.

And never in the ages that have passed,
Since this heroic act of love was done,
Has there a nobler deed of love been wrought,
A nobler victory over self been won.

Villiers de L'Isle Adam;

OR,

THE DEFENCE OF RHODES, A.D. 1522.

INTRODUCTION.

AMONG the many feats of arms done by the Knights of S. John—and their deeds of heroism will bear comparison with any which have ever been recorded in the world's history—none perhaps exceeds their glorious defence of Rhodes, in 1522, when a mere handful of men, led by these heroes, repelled the attacks of the vast Turkish host, led by the mighty Solyman, for six months.

SIX hundred knights, as bold and brave
    As e'er on land or sea*
Maintained the cause of truth and right
    In deeds of chivalry,

---

* The Knights of S. John had become as famous throughout Europe for their maritime skill as they had long been for their warlike renown.

Assembled at their master's call,
Counsel with him to hold
Touching a letter he had had
From Solyman the bold.

"My brethren," said L'Isle Adam,
"I must your counsel take,
When you this letter well have read,
What answer I shall make.
It is from Sultan Solyman,
Who hopes that I may reign
In glory and in happiness
In our beloved domain.

"Much do I fear that his fair words
No special favour bodes,
But that he seeks to drive us out
From our fair home in Rhodes.
He styles himself the king of kings,
And lord of all the sea ;
Tell me, shall we in answer say
We will his vassals be ?

"All Hungary he has overrun,
   And taken fair Belgrade;
The Christians he has put to death,
   Or worse, his captives made.
Congratulations from us now
   He courteously demands,
For all the conquests he has made
   Throughout these Christian lands.

"Close by the Holy Sepulchre,*
   Where our Lord's body lay
From Friday till He rose again
   On glorious Easter-day,
Our founders placed two hospitals,
   A refuge safe to be
For Christian pilgrims, who came there
   That holy place to see.

---

* In the middle of the eleventh century, about A.D. 1048, two hospitals, one for either sex, were erected at Jerusalem, near the Holy Sepulchre; that for the men was dedicated to S. John the Almoner, and that for the women to S. Mary Magdalene. From the first of these sprung the order of knights known as Knights Hospitallers, or Knights of S. John, and subsequently in history as Knights of Rhodes, and Knights of Malta.

" Through weal and woe, in peace or war,
  It has been, from that hour,
Our work to shield Christ's pilgrims true
  From the vile Turkish power.
Shall we now stop our glorious work,
  And bow beneath the sway
Of the great Sultan Solyman,
  And his behests obey?

" His courteous words are but a cloke
  To hide his hatred deep.
The Knights of Rhodes, he knows full well,
  Can ne'er his friendship keep;
For they are sworn, by sacred vow,
  Christ's pilgrims to defend
Against the desolating Turks,
  Even unto life's end.

" Their corsairs still infest our seas,
  And ever and again
We hear of cruel deeds of blood
  Done to unarmèd men;

But lately, as I came from France,
　Cartogli,* their great chief,
Would have surprised and captured us
　But for dark night's relief.

" My brethren, full well we know
　The Sultan's mighty power;
We must not keep it out of sight
　In this our trying hour.
Few forces have we to resist
　His overwhelming hosts,
Knights of S. John, are you prepared
　To perish at your posts?"

Thus spake Villiers de L'Isle Adam,
　And brightly gleamed his eye
As he gazed on his noble knights;
　Then raised it up on high,
As if his soul, loose from earth's ties,
　Stood ready for its flight,
From darksome shadows of this world,
　To Heaven's eternal light.

---

* The corsair Cartogli was hovering about Cape S. Angelo in
the hope of capturing L'Isle Adam, who managed to escape his
treacherous enemy under cover of the night.

And like a bright electric spark
  Went round that look of fire,
Kindling in many a hero's breast
  That thrilling strong desire
Which brave men feel, when danger lies
  In duty's sacred way,
And they have learnt, at that high call,
  To hear is to obey.

Then rose De Barbaran, from Spain.
  "Life is but short," said he,
"E'en though we live to grey old age,
  In full prosperity;
But honour lives beyond the grave,
  'Tis the great legacy
Which Christian knights are bound to leave
  To all posterity.

" Let us return a firm reply,
  Calmly and courteously;
For courtesy is ever due,
  E'en to an enemy;

But let the Sultan understand,
　　Though we all wish for peace,
Our vows are pledged, Christians to aid,
　　And captives to release."

" Manselle of France, what sayest thou ?"
　　" 'Twere deepest shame," said he,
" If we to Sultan Solyman
　　Sent words of sympathy.
Defenceless prisoners he has slain,
　　Basely and cruelly,
Because they would not at his word
　　JESUS their LORD deny.

" Fair Christian maidens he has led
　　Into captivity !
Oh, cruel fate, far worse than death,
　　Of deepest agony !
S. John's true knights must 'gainst such deeds
　　Fight with their latest breath,
Better than tolerate such deeds,
　　To die a soldier's death."

" Hussey* of England, tell us now
    What counsel thou dost give ;
Shall we defy great Solyman,
    Or by his favour live ?"
"Worthless is life," the brave knight said,
    " If it is bought with shame ;
At every cost, let us maintain
    The honour of our name.

" If heaven demand our lives, we know
    Those lives have long been given,
By sacred vow, to our great King,
    Reigning in highest heaven.
Death must come once to every man,
    To age, or youth, or beauty ;
Happy are they who get that call
    In the plain path of duty.

---

* Fr. Nicholas Hussey commanded the English bastion.
There were probably many English knights present at the siege.
The names of twenty only are preserved, and these knights
well sustained the honour of their country and their order.   It
is stated that they all died at the post of duty, and that the
English bastion had in consequence to be entrusted to knights
of other languages.

" Let us not send defiant words
   The Sultan to provoke,
For our poor brethren's sake, who lie
   Beneath his cruel yoke ;
But if he comes, with all his hosts,
   To force us to the fight,
Then let us all our duty do,
   And GOD defend the right."

Then rose the knights with one accord,
   And raised their swords on high,
And pledged their knightly words to live
   In honour, or to die.
" By GOD's great grace we will," said they,
   " True to our vows remain ;
We join in what the knights have said,
   From England, France, and Spain."

" Now GOD be praised," said L'Isle Adam,
   "For making us all one,
Able to say, for life or death,
   GOD's holy will be done.

Calmly prepared to meet the shock
　　Of the vast Turkish host,
Or else prepared, if GOD so wills,
　　To perish at our posts."

Again the knights are called to hear
　　Proud Solyman's reply
To the brave letter they had sent,
　　Calmly and courteously.
They knew their words had failed to change
　　The Sultan's fell decree,
To drive the knights of Rhodes forth from
　　Their island in the sea.

" My brethren," said L'Isle Adam,
　　" I call you here to-day,
To tell you that great Solyman
　　Is hither on his way.
Two hundred thousand men he has
　　Under his own command;
With these he purposes to take
　　Possession of our land.

"If we will yield at once, he swears,
  By Mahomet's great name,
To let us go in peace, and e'en
  His strong protection claim;
But if we dare resist his will,
  Then all our forts shall lie
Low as the grass, and all the knights
  By his strong sword shall die.

"Four thousand and five hundred men
  Are all the troops we have
Wherewith to meet great Solyman,
  And his fierce onset brave.
Shall we resist, or shall we yield?"
  A shout, as with one breath,
Came from the knights, who loudly cried,
  "Let us fight to the death!"

The gathering storm soon burst in force
  On the heroic band,
Who had for Christ's true pilgrims fought
  In many a foreign land.

Their faith was strong, their hearts were brave,
  As in the days gone by;
All were resolved, in this great fray,
  To conquer or to die.

With wondrous skill new forts were raised,
  And all, with willing hearts,
In this great preparation work
  Did their appointed parts.
The old forts too were strengthened well,
  For well worked every man,
A warm reception to accord
  To Sultan Solyman.

And now the galleys of the knights,
  Cruising around the coast,
Report the Turkish admiral*
  Approaching with his host.
And soon a well-known signal fire†
  From Mount S. Stephen's height

---

* The pirate Cartogli was appointed by Solyman Admiral of the Fleet.

† Early in the morning of the 26th June, 1522, a signal from Mount Saint Stephen intimated to the Rhodians that the Turkish fleet was in sight. Countless sails studded the Lycian Strait.

Proclaims that the vast Turkish fleet
　Is coming into sight.

More than four hundred sail are seen
　Studding the Lycian Strait,
And proudly standing towards the shore
　In pomp and martial state.
The people crowd the city walls
　To view the grand array;*
And many hearts are filled with grief,
　But no hearts with dismay.

Cara Mohammed,† admiral
　Of the great Turkish fleet,

---

* The whole population hurried to the ramparts and towers to behold the terrible armament that threatened them with destruction. Four hundred sail swept past the mouth of the haven with the pomp and circumstance of a triumphal pageant.

† The Vice-Admiral, Cara Mohammèd, when he arrived off the entrance of the bay, ordered his galleys to strike sail and row into the port. The rowers accordingly stretched to their oars; and the Rhodians, conceiving their harbour in danger, rushed with noble emulation to the seaward bastion. But a few cannon-balls deterred the Turk from persevering in his bravado; and the Rhodians, proudly waving their standard,. shouted in scorn and triumph as he bore away.

Recklessly rows into the port,
  His enemies to greet.
The Rhodians fire a grand salute
  From their great seaward wall ;
But every cannon on this day
  Is loaded with a ball.

The Turks, though brave, cannot remain
  Under this deadly fire.
Cheer upon cheer rings from the wall,
  As they in haste retire.
They see they have to deal with men
  Fully resolved to die,
Rather than sacrifice their faith,
  Their home, or liberty.

Though they retreat, 'tis but to find
  A place upon the coast
Where they can land their warlike stores,
  And all their martial host,
And soon against the inland wall
  Thunders the iron hail,
To make a breach through which the Turks
  The city may assail.

A breach is made, and from the walls
   Is seen the fierce array
Of chosen men, who through the breach
   Resolve to fight their way.
Oh, gallant knights and soldiers brave,
   Ye must be calm and bold,
More numerous are these chosen men
   Than all your force thrice told.

L'Isle Adam his small force reviews.
   "Soldiers of Christ," said he,
"Our trial-day is come at last;
   Behold the enemy.
Few are the words I need now speak
   Your stedfast souls to move,
Now is the time for gallant deeds
   Your chivalry to prove.

"Yet, brethren, let us not forget
   Where true strength ever lies,
When our small band is compassed round
   With countless enemies.

'Christ lives, Christ reigns, and Christ commands,'*
Was the old battle-cry,
Which nerved the Christian knights of old
    In many a victory.

" 'Christ lives, Christ reigns, and Christ commands,'
    Be this our cry to day,
When with our cruel foes, the Turks,
    We join in deadly fray.
Christ lives, therefore in death is life,
    Christ reigns, our King is He,
And Christ commands, His will be done,
    Now and eternally."

Bravely the Moslems forward move,
    To take the town by storm;
Calmly the knights, under their chief,
    In fighting order form;

---

* This was the war-cry of the Christian soldiers at the battle
of Jaffa, A.D. 1119, when Baldwin, king of Jerusalem, followed
by Du Puis and his Hospitallers, altogether one hundred and
sixty knights, rushed into the very thickest ranks of the enemy,
turned the tide of battle, and won a great victory.

They do not wait until their foes
    The city ramparts gain,
But sally forth, in close array,
    To meet them on the plain.

"With faith within, and steel without" *
    They rush upon the foe,
Wherever knights of Rhodes are seen
    Moslems are lying low.
Nought can resist their fiery charge,
    Or check them in the fight,
They break the Turkish battle line,
    And put their troops to flight.

The bells ring out in old S. John's,
    And thousands hurry there,
To praise God for the victory,
    And to uplift a prayer

---

* "At the cry of battle," says S. Bernard, "they armed themselves with faith within, and steel without. They feared neither the number nor the fury of the barbarians. They were proud to conquer, happy to die for Jesus Christ, and believed that every victory came from God."—See MICHAUD'S *History of the Crusades,* and S. BERNARD'S *Exhortatio ad Milites Templi.*

For the repose of those brave men
  Who, in the deadly fray,
Had, in the cause of Christ their Lord,
  Fallen upon this day.

The Moslems still press on the siege,
  But numbers daily fall
In sorties by the knights of Rhodes,
  Or cannon from the wall,
Until with longing eyes they look
  Back on the Lycian shore,
And words of mutiny are heard,
  To press the siege no more.

When the report reached Solyman
  That his choice soldiery
Had, in the hour of their defeat,
  Said words of mutiny;
With fifteen thousand chosen troops
  He seeks the front again,
And, in his fiery anger, swears
  To decimate the men.

"Cowards, stand forth !" he fiercely says ;
  "Dishonoured should I be,
Did I not mete sharp punishment
  For your foul mutiny.
One man in every ten shall die,
  Thus will I cleanse your stain,
Ere I consent to lead you forth
  To meet your foes again !

"Shame on you, Moslem soldiery,
  Like cowards thus to fly,
You, whom so often I have led
  To glorious victory !
As for myself, here I remain
  To conquer yonder town,
Or else my empire and my life
  Together to lay down."

The mutineers, with shame and grief,
  Thought their last hour was nigh.
"Great Sultan, pardon us," said they,
  "Once more our valour try."

"Respite, I grant," said Solyman,
    "In answer to your prayer;
But do you see those battlements?
    Win your full pardon there."

A shout bursts from the Turkish troops,
    Now burning with desire
To cleanse their stain, and glory gain
    Under the Christians' fire.
" Lead us again against our foes,"
    Tumultuously they cry,
" And we will drive them from the walls,
    Or in the effort die."

The siege-works now are brought quite near
    To the old city wall;
But deadly is the Rhodian fire,
    And hundreds daily fall;
Assault upon assault is made,
    But all are made in vain.
The knights of Rhodes, though thinned in ranks,
    Their city still retain.

But, ah ! what means that fearful noise,
    Which thunders through the town ?
The Turks have sprung a hidden mine,
    The English tower is down ;
The brave knights guarding it are dead,
    The Turks are drawing nigh,
They rush in through the open breach,
    Shouting their battle cry.

What is that ensign on the fort?
    It is the Turkish flag.
Mount, knights, mount, Rhodians, to the height,
    Tear down the cursed rag.
Where is the master, L'Isle Adam ?
    Where are his knights so brave?
To rescue ! oh, to rescue come,
    And our dear city save !

Before the altar, where he knelt,
    L'Isle Adam heard that cry,
For he was praying in the church
    Mary of victory ;

He rushes forth, and heads the knights,
  Who rally at his call,
And fiercely charges at the Turks
  Upon the city wall.

He seizes a scalading spear,
  And, midst the deafening din,
Dashes through smoke and musket balls
  The bastion height to win ;
For there he sees a Turkish flag
  Defiling the old town,
With his own hand he seizes it,
  And tears the ensign down.

"Christ lives, Christ reigns, and Christ commands,"
  Shouted the gallant knight,
As he again the Christian flag
  Plants on the bastion height ;
The Christian soldiers forward rush
  At the inspiring cry,
Each one resolved, in Christ's dear cause,
  To conquer or to die.

The Moslems quail before that charge,
　And, wavering, backward reel;
They cannot stand that withering fire,
　That wall of living steel.
Dire panic strikes them as they hear
　The Christian battle cry;
"Charge home, charge home," cries L'Isle Adam,
　"Behold, they fly, they fly!"

Two thousand Turks die in the breach,
　Victims in this dread fight.
Alas! the knights of Rhodes have lost
　Full many a gallant knight.
Guyot de Marselhac is slain,
　And Chevalier Manselle,
Their pledge to die for JESUS' sake
　They have redeemed right well.

For five long months the siege is pressed
　Against the goodly town,
By mine and cannon, day and night,
　The forts are broken down;

But still the knights in every breach
　The enemy defy,
They none of them know how to yield,
　They all know how to die.

The wall of steel is ever there
　To meet the advancing host;
The knights fulfil their plighted words,
　And perish at their posts.
Wherever danger lies, be sure
　Knights of S. John are found,
Fighting and dying gallantly,
　But never giving ground.

The Sultan broods within his tent,
　In anger, pride, and grief;
He fears that Christian states at last
　Will send the knights relief.
" Full eighty thousand men," he says,
　" Have died in this campaign ;
Must I the beaten remnant take
　To Asia's shores again ?

" Have all my generals been brave ?
　Have my troops been in fault ?

How is it that they all have failed
  In every great assault ?
'Twould shake my empire to take back
  My troops in grief and shame ;
It cannot be, I must not soil
  The lustre of my name.

" Yet winter rapidly draws on ;
  It soon will be too late
To save my army and myself
  From a disastrous fate.
For should relief at last be brought
  To those heroic men,
We ne'er, perchance, shall safely reach
  The Lycian shore again."

A traitor seeks the Sultan's tent ; *
  Oh, ask not for his name !
Let it lie buried in the grave
  With his eternal shame !

---

* The Sultan was seriously meditating the abandonment of the
siege, when this Albanian deserter informed him of the terrible
straits to which the garrison of Rhodes was reduced. —See
FLEURY'S *Hist. Eccl.*

"Most noble prince," the recreant says,
"Nothing can now restrain
Your troops from taking yonder town,
If they attack again.

"Most of the knights of Rhodes are dead,
And many wounded lie,
Only a remnant now remains
Of the brave soldiery.
Disease and famine are at work
Within the leaguered town,
The walls, the towers, the battlements,
Have all been broken down."

Before the bastion of Auvergne
An envoy now draws nigh,
With letter from great Solyman,
Requesting a reply.
He sends to offer generous terms
Of life and royal grace,
If the knights will capitulate,
And yield the shattered place.

" These are the words," said L'Isle Adam,
    " Which we send in reply :
The knights and soldiers in this town
    Are all prepared to die,
If the boon is not granted them
    Their well-loved town to save ;
They can at least beneath its stones
    Lie in an honoured grave."

But now a sad procession stands
    Before the palace door,
Matrons and youthful maidens fair,
    Children and aged poor.
" Oh, listen, noble L'Isle Adam,"
    They suppliantly cry,
" Suffer us not in pain and shame
    By the vile Turks to die.

" You and your band of gallant knights
    Have hitherto prevailed,
When you have been by countless foes
    Incessantly assailed.

But now our walls are lying low,
   Half of our troops are slain;
Who can drive back the Turkish hosts
   When they assault again?

" Sad will it be for us to fall
   Beneath the Moslem power;
God only knows our agony
   In this heartrending hour.
But if the Sultan offers terms,
   Honour and life to spare,
Oh, when you send him your reply
   Think of our humble prayer!"

And now the saintly Bishop speaks,
   In his loved people's name:
" Villiers de L'Isle Adam," said he,
   "Covered thou art with fame;
Noble has been thy grand defence
   Of this beleagured town,
Posterity will deck thy name
   With an undying crown.

" But look, my noble prince, on Him
    Who left the crown of heaven
To suffer here below and die,
    That we might be forgiven.
Think of *His* pain, *His* grief, *His* shame,
    And that tremendous price
Which, to redeem us from our sins,
    He paid in sacrifice.

" He died that we might live; will you
    Live that we may not die?
Honour says, ' Die upon the breach ;'
    Does Christ say that on high?
Does He not say, ' Let all give way
    To the great law of love?
Rule not your deeds by this world's laws,
    But by the laws above.'

" Tis great to die a soldier's death,
    'Tis greater still to live,
If by your living you to these
    Honour and life can give.

E

Oh, choose the greater sacrifice !
Do what your LORD would say,
'Christ lives, Christ reigns, and Christ commands,'
Be that your rule to-day."

And now the knights meet once again—
Not as they met before,
Six hundred strong ; they number now
Two hundred and four score.
And midst this remnant of the brave,
Not one knight can be found
Who, in the long defence of Rhodes,
Has not received a wound.

" We know," said they, " brave L'Isle Adam,
Why you have called us here,
It is that we may every one
The Sultan's message hear.
We all keep to our great resolve,
In this great cause to die ;
Only o'er Christian corpses shall
Turks march to victory."

" My brethren," said L'Isle Adam,
    " Our lives we count as loss ;
By vow they have been given to Him
    Who died upon the cross.
A glorious death, such as our friends
    And brother-knights have won,
Is the most fitting end for us,
    Knights of the great S. John.

" But ' Christ commands ;' what is *His* will?
    Oh, how this tries my heart !
'Tis easy with this suffering life,
    And all its cares, to part ;
But life and death belong to Him ;
    Is it His holy will
That we should, for our brethren's sake,
    Bear our life's burden still ?

" The Sultan swears, if we will yield,
    Our citizens to spare ;
Their honour, life, and liberty
    Shall be his special care.

If we resist, he also swears,
By his most solemn word,
That every soul within the town
Shall perish by the sword.

" Most carefully have I enquired
If we can still defend
The city we have held so well,
To a successful end.
But all report that, with our walls
And bastions broken down,
We cannot, with our scanty troops,
Still hold the ruined town.

" And you, brave sharers of my toil,
Are all the knights I have
Of the six hundred who at first
Pledged life this town to save.
It may be Christ has spared our lives
To offer as the price
Which we, for our dear brethren's sake,
Must give in sacrifice."

Then all the knights with one accord
    Knelt at S. Mary's shrine,
And said, "O JESUS, Mary's Son,
    We have no will but Thine !
We bow our heads to Thy blest will,
    Whatever that may be,
In shame or grief, in life or death,
    Now and eternally."

"Christ reigns !" He has the empire gained
    Over that manly pride
Which would have led the gallant knights
    In glory to have died.
He shows them a still higher way
    Their chivalry to prove,
Eclipsing glory here on earth
    With glory from above.

For now they see self-sacrifice
    Is chivalry's true root—
That no act has the royal stamp
    Unless it bears *this* fruit.

To die in glory in the breach
Looks noble, great, and high ;
To live, others to aid and save,
Is truer chivalry.

Rhodes falls ; but the great Solyman
Fulfils his plighted word :
No citizens are prisoners made,
None perish by the sword.
Matrons and maidens, children weak,
Honour and life retain ;
Freedom is given to all alike,
To leave or to remain.

The churches all protected are,
By Christians still retained ;
The Sultan gives his royal word
They shall not be profaned.
The knights may all in honour leave,
And all their arms retain,
To seek in other lands and climes
Fresh glories to obtain.

And now the Sultan asks to see
  The hero so well tried,
Who with his knights for five long months
  His army has defied.
An officer of fitting rank
  To L'Isle Adam is sent ;
To ask him to meet Solyman
  Within the royal tent.

The warriors met ; so calm and brave,
  So noble, great, and high ;
Looked L'Isle Adam on this sad day
  Of his adversity,
It won the youthful despot's heart—
  " Oh, gallant knight," said he,
" Listen now to the boon I ask
  In full sincerity.

" Thy fallen fortunes join to mine,
  My friend and counsellor be,
No dignity within my realm
  I deem too high for thee ;

For thou hast won a hero's name,
  Though thou hast lost this town.
Oh, let that name to mine be joined,
  A jewel in my crown !"

"Most noble prince," said L'Isle Adam,
  "My plighted faith is given
To serve the King, who died for me,
  Reigning in highest heaven ;
And next, to rule those noble knights
  Who lately in this town
Have, by their brave, heroic deeds,
  Increased their old renown.

"If all the kingdoms of this world
  Were freely offered me—
If I would stain my grey old age
  With such deep treachery,
How poor would be the great reward,
  How full of misery,
Through what remains of this brief life,
  And through eternity !

" And could you trust a recreant knight
   Who for the love of gain
Could leave his brave and noble knights,
   And his soul's honour stain ?
Or could you trust a Christian man,
   False to his plighted word,
False to himself, false to his faith,
   His Saviour, and his LORD ?

" Since Rhodes has fallen, mighty prince,
   I thank GOD heartily
It is to one who in success
   Can show sweet clemency.
Fix well this jewel in thy crown,
   It will shine pure and bright
When conquest and proud victories
   Sink in oblivion's night."

The glare of many victories
   Shone round the Sultan's way,
As mighty nations he subdued
   Beneath his sovereign sway ;

But brighter shines in honour's page
That brave, heroic man,
Grand Master of the Knights of Rhodes—
Villiers de L'Isle Adam.

The defence of Rhodes, which covered its defenders with
glory, was to the sovereigns of Europe a subject of the deepest
shame. For two hundred years the Knights Hospitallers had
maintained this last bulwark in the East. Once during that
period they had successfully resisted the whole might of the
Turkish Empire; and the defence of Rhodes had become a by-
word of admiration throughout Europe. The feeling of the
world was aptly expressed by Charles V., who, upon hearing of
the disastrous issue of the siege, turned to his courtiers, and
exclaimed, "There has been nothing so well lost in the world as
Rhodes."—See PORTER'S *History of the Knights of Malta.*

Divisions among the Christian sovereigns of Europe, arising
out of private jealousies and ambitious designs, prevented them
from sending the help which they were in honour bound to do
to the gallant heroes, who dared with four thousand five hundred
men to withstand the shock of two hundred thousand Turks, led
by the mighty Solyman, and who succeeded, incredible as it may
appear, in keeping them at bay for six months. Had it not
been for treachery the Turks would probably never have taken
Rhodes.

Holy Church.

ONWARD through the rolling ages
　　Holy Church pursues her way,
Training martyrs, saints, and sages,
　　For their home of endless day.

The Church endures throughout all time.

Calling sinners to repentance,
　　Telling them of that vast love
Which, to sanctify and save them,
　　Brought down Jesus from above.

Her thirst for the conversion of sinners.

Holy Church is Christ's own Body,
　　She loves souls for whom He died;
All her labours are to bring us
　　To our Saviour crucified.

The Church Christ's Body. Her longing to bring souls to Jesus.

First in infancy she takes us,
　　And applies the precious blood,
Blotting out the sin of Adam
　　In the blest baptismal flood.

Holy Baptism.

Christian education.

Then she leads us as God's children
Through this world of sin and pain,
Aiding us in life's long battle,
Till our Saviour comes again.

Confirmation.

As the time of danger thickens
Round our inexperienced days,
Confirmation gifts she brings us,
Strengthening us in duty's ways.

The power of confirmation gifts.

Be courageous, Christian soldier,
Bravely wage thy holy strife,
By the help of God the Spirit
Thou canst gain eternal life.

The power of overcoming sin,

Oh, bethink thee, when temptation
Gathers round thee like a flood,
Thou may'st stem the evil torrent
Through the power of Jesus' blood!

Through faith in Christ.

Onward, though thy foes be many,
Strike them down in Christ's great name;
Trust Him, He will give thee victory
Over Satan, sin, and shame.

Then, O wonder far exceeding
    What by words can e'er be said,
Jesus, our incarnate Saviour,
    Comes to be our daily bread.

Spiritual food.

See, before the holy altar,
    God's commissioned priest doth stand,
Offering up the dread oblation,
    Which our Saviour did command.

The Oblation.

Now midst reverend ceremonial
    Sounds the awful liturgy,
Which upraises earthly creatures
    Christ's own flesh and blood to be.

Consecration.

Bow the head in adoration,
    Worship thy incarnate Lord ;
Banish hence all vain disputings,
    Simply trust thy Saviour's word.

*With angels
and archangels
worship Jesus.*

Draw ye near in faith unfeignèd,
    Contrite heart, and fervent love ;
Feed upon Christ's Blood and Body,
    Living food from heaven above.

*Holy Com-
munion.*

How shall man, with guilt oppressèd,
    Such dread mysteries draw nigh?
How approach the Pure and Holy,
    Bending from His throne on high?

Is thy conscience deeply burdened,
    Bowed to earth with guilty stains?
Hast thou sinned against that Saviour,
    Who for thee endured sin's pains?

Ah! His mercy still can reach thee,
    Still He yearns thy soul to win;
In His Church is still provision
    For the pardon of thy sin.

Seek God's priest in deep contrition,
    All thy secret griefs reveal;
Make a true and full confession,
    Nor one conscious sin conceal.

Thus again shall peace and pardon
    Reach thee through the precious blood,
And thy Saviour's absolution
    Shall thy soul with fresh joy flood.

Then in awe, but not in terror, Doubts removed.
    Seek the Eucharistic food ;
Eat the living bread from heaven,
    Drink the saving, cleansing blood.

Thus refreshed, pursue thy journey, The soul
    In the strength of that blest meat, strengthened
and refreshed.
Till thy pilgrimage is ended,
    And thy soul for heaven made meet.

And when earthly things are passing, Visitation of
the sick.
    And eternal things are nigh,
Holy Church still watches o'er us,
    Waits to catch our latest sigh ;

Waits to nurse her suffering children Commendatory
office.
    Through their latest agony ;
Calmly gives their souls to Jesus,
    As they flutter, and are free.

Then, like mother, true and faithful, Burial of the
dead.
    By a tender instinct led,
Reverently she lays our bodies
    In their consecrated bed.

The body left
in God's
keeping.
And with words of meek submission,

Christian hope, in suffering born,

Leaves them safe in God's own keeping

Till the resurrection morn.

Jesus, not to dark confusion
  Let me wake on that dread day ;
Bid me not depart with sinners
  From Thy presence blest away.

But in mercy call me near Thee,
  Let me hear those words of love—
" Come, ye children of my Father,
  Enter on the joys above."

The Church
reigns through-
out eternity.
Onward through the eternal ages

  Christ's triumphant Church shall reign,

Free from every spot or wrinkle,

  Cleansed from every guilty stain.

Advent.

INSTANTIS ADVENTUM DEI.

(PARIS BREVIARY.)

Jesu, thine Advent from the skies
We now await with anxious eyes;
May we to meet Thee all prepare,
With hymns of praise and fervent prayer.

The eternal Son of God Most High
Consents to lay His glory by,
To save man from sin's endless doom;
He spurneth not the Virgin's womb.

He cometh! merciful and meek:
Zion, arise, thy King to seek!
Close not thine heart against His call,
Who offers heavenly peace to all.

F

As Judge of all, in clouds of light,
Soon shall He break upon our sight,
And bear on high His members blest
To their eternal place of rest.

Let sin and deeds of darkness fly,
Ere Christ, the Light of Light, draws nigh ;
And, as the old Adam hence departs,
The new be formed within our hearts.

To Jesus, who came down from heaven
That fallen man might be forgiven,
To Father, and to Spirit blest,
Be praise eternally addressed.

VERBUM SUPERNUM PRODIENS.

ETERNAL Word, true Light of Light,
Begotten of the Father's might—
Whose birth this fallen world renewed
As time its downward course pursued—

Our hearts illumine from above,
Oh, let them burn with thy blest love,
That when Thy voice we hear again,
No deeds of shame our souls may stain.

And when, just Judge, Thou drawest nigh
All deeds to scrutinize and try,
Rendering to secret sins their due,
A kingdom to Thy faithful few,

Let us not from Thy face be driven,
For sins unmourned and unforgiven;
But grant us places with the blest,
In holy and eternal rest.

Glory and honour, praise and laud,
To the one undivided God,
To Father, Son, and Paraclete,
Now and through ages infinite.

Christmas Old and New.

"I remember the days of old."—*Psalm* cxliii. 5.

As through the vista of past years
I muse upon old Christmas joys,
When we, and those now passed away,
Together lived as girls and boys,
And gathered round the old fireside,
To keep our happy Christmas-tide,—

Unbidden tears my eyes bedew,
For love still burns within my heart
Towards those who round the cheerful hearth
In our home pleasures took their part,
And joined in carols sweet to sing—
Glory to Christ, the new-born King.

Whatever joys may yet remain
To cheer us on life's toilsome way,
Past joys can ne'er come back again,
The olden days are gone for aye;

Yet the old faces still seem near,
Living in love's bright memory clear.

Yet let us not in sadness mourn
For those whom God has called away
To taste those joys in Paradise,
Which never lessen or decay—
Joys, purified from all alloy,
Which rolling years can ne'er destroy.

Around us still are loving hearts,
Full of simplicity and truth,
Learning old England's Christmas ways,
In the bright sunshine of their youth ;
We must not overcloud their way,
On this their happy Christmas-day.

''Twere selfish not to share the mirth
Of younger hearts, because our own
Live in the past with those we loved,
In days which never can return :
Self must not hold our souls in thrall
To-day, when Christ was born for all.

And if our thoughts will backward fly
O'er years of mingled joy and pain;
Will linger round the old fireside,
And bring the loved ones back again;
Oh, let us think we still are one
In Jesus, God's eternal Son!

In spirit they are with us still,
United in sweet bonds of love—
We in the Church of Christ on earth,
They in the glorious Church above;
Finding our common joy in One,
Jesus, sweet Mary's new-born Son.

All joys of earth soon pass away;
Oh, may we know the joy at last
Of sitting in our heavenly home
With those we loved in the dim past,
And those with whom, in the old way,
We keep our Christmas feast to-day.

The Babe of Bethlehem.

"Let us now go even unto Bethlehem, and see this thing which is come to pass."—*S. Luke* ii. 15.

CHRISTIANS, come to Bethlehem
　　At this holy season;
Not to come to Jesus now
　　Would be faithless treason.

Gaze upon the infant God,
　　In His manger sleeping;
Joseph and the mother-maid
　　Solemn vigil keeping.

Wondrous is the mystery
　　Of this beauteous vision;
And how glorious the part
　　Of that Virgin's mission.

'Tis to nurture that sweet child,
    Which to her is given,
Nurse Him who, though born of her,
    Is the King of heaven.

See the Infant opes His eyes,
    On His mother gazing ;
Reverently the Virgin bends,
    Her beloved one raising.

Now she folds Him in her arms,
    Her dear child caressing ;
Now she utters tender words,
    Her sweet child addressing.

Now she lifts Him up on high,
    On His features gazing ;
Rapturous love o'erwhelms her soul
    At the sight amazing.

Take thy fill of joy, pure maid ;
    Graces without measure
Have thy holy soul prepared,
    To embrace thy treasure.

Thou canst gaze upon thy God
  As none other creature ;
For in thee no sin has stamped
  Its defiling feature.

Oh, dear Jesu, Mary's Son,
  From Thy manger lowly,
Make us loving, meek, and pure,
  Like Thy mother, holy ;

That, like her, when life is past,
  And fulfilled our mission,
We may gaze upon Thy face
  In the heavenly vision.

Jesu, Son of God most High,
  Jesu, Son of Mary,
Of Thy praises, God and man,
  May we never weary.

The Desire of all Nations.

"The Desire of all nations shall come."—*Haggai* ii. 7.

HE is come, He is come, the desire of all nations,
For whom faithful watchmen have kept their long
 stations ;
Yea, come to fulfil what prophets foretold
Of Him and His mission, in ages of old.

He is come, He is come, the one great Restorer,
Whom God's Church had ever been keeping before her
As One who should save His people from sin,
And for them a happy eternity win.

He is come, He is come, the angels are singing,
The æther with heavenly music is ringing ;
All glory to God in the Highest be given,
And peace toward man from the Father in heaven.

He is come, He is come.   Oh, see the light gleaming,
With heavenly radiance around the earth streaming !
The shepherds are filled with awe and affright
Whilst o'er their flocks watching at dead of the night.

He is come, He is come. Oh, shepherds, why tarry,
When you to your fellows such tidings may carry?
To Bethlehem fly, and visit your God;
He lies in a manger upon the cold sod.

He is come, He is come. Lo ! kneeling before Him
Are Joseph and Mary, who meekly adore Him,
And pay Him on earth the praise which is given
By myriads of angels in the highest heaven.

He is come, He is come; the bright star is guiding
The kings of the east to the place of His biding:
The manger they reach—the home of His birth,
To worship the Maker of heaven and earth.

He is come, He is come. Oh, chant forth His glory;
In carols and anthems proclaim the glad story;
Yea, sweetly repeat, again and again,
That God is incarnate, and dwells among men.

He is come, He is come, the one great oblation
Ordained before time to procure man's salvation :
All shadows have passed, all things are made new
In Jesus our Saviour, the Sacrifice true.

The Old, Old Song.

"Glory to God in the highest, and on earth peace, good will toward men."—*Luke* ii. 14.

OH, sing again the old, old song—
Old and yet ever new ;
So full of mystery and love,
And yet so simply true ;
How Jesus, Son of God Most High,
Enthroned in highest heaven,
Became a babe in Bethlehem,
That man might be forgiven.

Mary, the ever-blessèd Maid,
Chosen by God's decree
To be the mother of her Lord,
From all eternity,
Came to the royal town, foretold
By true prophetic word
To be the natal-place of Christ,
Our Saviour and our Lord.

Have they no room for thee, fair maid?
  Canst thou not find a bed
In all the inns of Bethlehem,
  To rest thy weary head?
Must thou, higher in dignity
  Then all the queens of earth,
Be driven to a cattle-shed,
  To give thy Saviour birth?

'Tis even so.   God seeth not
  As sinful man doth see;
He measures not by outward marks
  The place of dignity.
To Him, the noblest place on earth
  Was that poor cattle-shed,
Where Mary, for her Son Divine,
  Selected her poor bed.

Oh, wondrous is the mystery
  Shown in this humble birth—
The Infant in fair Mary's arms
  Is God of heaven and earth!
The eternal Son, in human flesh,   ˙
  As man with men doth dwell;

His name this blessed truth proclaims :
JESUS—IMMANUEL.

Who can express the rapturous joy,
    O Mother undefiled !
Which filled thee with adoring love,
    In gazing on thy Child ?
The mighty King of heaven and earth
    Lies on the lowly sod ;
Thy true and only Son, and yet
    Thy Maker and thy God.

Sing out your anthems bright and clear,
    Ye heavenly choirs on high ;
Oh that some strains might reach our souls
    Of your sweet minstrelsy !
Oh that your love might tune our hearts
    With heavenly joy, to sing
The praises of this wondrous child,
    Our Saviour and our King !

The holy shepherds as they watched
    Heard your celestial song,
As in rich harmonies ye filled
    The welkin all along.

Glory to God on high, ye sang,
  Peace and good will toward men,
So we, on this bright Christmas-tide,
  Will chant these words again.

And as the shepherds hasted on,
  Their new-born King to greet,
And bowed in adoration due
  Before His sacred feet;
So may we ever seek Thee, Lord,
  In all the ways here given,
Until at last we worship Thee
  For evermore in heaven.

Then shall we join angelic choirs,
  And learn those glorious lays
Which ring throughout the heavenly courts
  To Thy eternal praise.
Then shall we see Thee as Thou art,
  In all Thy glory bright,
O Father, Son, and Holy Ghost,
  The uncreated Light.

The Christmas Tree.

"Out of the mouth of babes and sucklings Thou hast perfected praise."—*S. Matthew* xxi. 16.

" LITTLE one, why art thou singing so merrily
  Under the Christmas-tree?
Why is thy joyous voice ringing so cheerily?
  What fills thy heart with glee?"
"Sir, I am singing about blessèd Jesus,
  Born on this day for me ;
That is the reason I carol so merrily
  Under the Christmas-tree."

"Who is this Jesus who thus thy heart raises?
  Where was He born for thee?
Why dost thou love thus to sing out His praises?
  What has He done for thee?"
"Jesus is God, sir, and lived up in heaven
  In glorious majesty ;
Angels and archangels loved and adored Him,
  Holy and happy was He.

" But though so happy He did not forget me,
    One day His child to be ;
He loved and thought of me back in the ages
    Of past eternity.
From highest heaven He came down to seek me ;
    Great was His love, you see ;
Therefore I joyfully sing out His praises
    Under the Christmas-tree.

" Jesus was born in Bethlehem's fair city,
    As spake the prophecy ;
Not in a palace or any grand dwelling,
    But in deep poverty.
Mary, the Virgin, so holy and blessèd,
    Was, by God's high decree,
Chosen and fitted before all His creatures
    Jesus' dear Mother to be.

" There was no room found throughout all the city,
    Where holy Mary could be,
Therefore with Joseph she went to a stable,
    Where Christ was born for me.

G

Was He not good to give up all His glory
    And heavenly majesty,
And to come down to us, poor, meek, and lowly,
    Our dear Saviour to be?

"Shepherds then hastened to visit our Saviour
    Whilst yet a little baby;
Angels had told them where they should find Jesus,
    And His sweet Mother Mary.
Oh, how they wondered to find in a manger
    Him whom they came to see!
Yet in devotion they knelt down before Him,
    Owning Him Christ to be.

" Next came wise men from a very far country,
    Judah's great King to see,
Bringing Him presents of gold, myrrh, and incense,
    As their choice offerings free.
Though in a stable, and laid in a manger,
    They knew His high degree;
We too must own Him our God, King, and Saviour,
    And serve Him faithfully.

" I cannot tell you all that our Lord Jesus
   Did in His love so free,
How He endured pain, and death at last suffered
   On the mount Calvary.
Now He has risen and gone up to heaven ;
   But still He thinks of me,
And longs to have me there with Him in glory
   Through all eternity.

" Father and mother, and brothers and sisters,
   Jesus, my Lord, gives me ;
My home in this world, and my bright home in heaven,
   And gifts from the Christmas-tree.
Oh, then I must love my blessèd Lord Jesus
   For all His love to me,
And sing His praises out gladly and merrily
   Under the Christmas-tree !"

" Sing out thy carol, my bright little singer,
   In sweetest melody ;
Well hast thou told me the story of Jesus,
   And all His love so free.

Jesus was born to bring all men salvation,
  For me as well as for thee ;
Therefore together His praises we 'll carol,
  Under the Christmas-tree."

Glory and honour, dominion and power,
  Be, blessèd Lord, to Thee,
For all the mercy and love which Thou shewest
  In Thy nativity.
Ah ! may we ever, as time floweth onward,
  Thy faithful children be ;
And at last taste all the blessings we sing about,
  Under the Christmas-tree.

S. John the Evangelist.

"He lying on Jesus' breast."—*St. John* xiii. 25.

THOU favoured saint of God,
Oh, what a joy was thine,
As thou on Jesus' breast
Didst lovingly recline,

And on His face divine
Didst gaze in rapturous bliss,
Tasting the heavenly joy
Of such a love as His !

Friend of the incarnate Word,
'Twas thine, with love's keen eye,
To pierce the awful depths
Of His divinity.

'Twas thine, beneath the Cross,
To see the mingled tide
Of water and of blood
Flow from His sacred side.

S. John the Evangelist.

'Twas thine the charge to take
Of her who gave Him birth,
Who, though her very Son,
Is God of heaven and earth.

Thou favoured saint of God,
These special gifts were thine,
Because thy soul was cleansed
By love's pure fire divine.

O Jesu, living Source,
From whence pure love doth flow,
Grant that this cleansing fire
Within our hearts may glow;

That, freed from earthly stain,
And sharers of Thy love,
We may at last attain
Love's resting-place above.

S. John the Evangelist.

EUCHARISTIC.

"After this I looked, and, behold, a door was opened in
heaven."—*Rev.* iv. 1.
"And I beheld, and, lo, in the midst of the throne . . . . stood
a Lamb as it had been slain."—*Rev.* v. 6.

GLORIOUS was the heavenly vision
　　Which the loved apostle saw,
As, in rapturous love, his spirit
　　Broke its prison bars below,
And by Jesus' special grace
　　Ranged through realms of endless space.

Lo ! before the throne in heaven
　　He beheld the Lamb again,
Whom he faithfully had followed
　　Through this earthly life of pain,
Pleading by the precious price
　　Of His spotless sacrifice—

Pleading by His sacred passion,
    For the souls He died to save :
"Oh, My Father, through My merits
    Grant them victory o'er the grave ;
Grant them grace to conquer sin,
    And eternal glory win !"

Lamb of God, by faith we see Thee
    Pleading thus before the throne,
Shewing forth Thy death and passion
    Our transgressions to atone :
Through Thy spotless sacrifice
    Bring us, Lord, to Paradise.

Hymns of Penitence.

THE PENITENT'S LIFE AND LIGHT.

"In Him was life; and the life was the light of men."
S. John i. 4.

Jesu, Thou art the Life and Light
   Of every contrite heart!
Shed on my soul Thy radiance bright,
   Thy quickening life impart.

Long has my heart been held in thrall
   By things of sense and time;
But now, O Lord, that heart recall,
   And make it wholly Thine.

Ruined and desolate I lie,
   Without Thy saving grace:
Oh, hear my penitential cry!
   Turn not away Thy face,

But look on me with pity, Lord,
　Or who that look dare see?
Oh, speak that sweet absolving word—
　" Pardon, I died for Thee !"

To Father, Son, and Holy Ghost,
　The God whom we adore,
Be glory, as it was of old,
　And shall be evermore.　Amen.

THE CLEANSER OF THE TEMPLE.

"Create in me a clean heart, O God; and renew a right spirit
within me."—*Psalm* li. 10.

MERCIFUL Saviour, hear my prayer;
Oh, come and purify this heart,
Which longs to love Thee more and more,
And never from Thy love depart!

Evil defiles Thy temple, Lord,
Therefore in patient love draw nigh;
Purge me, but with long-suffering grace,
Come not in anger, lest I die.

But come in patient love, dear Lord—
Such love as Thou hast ever shown
To burdened sinners, such as I,
Who to Thy mercy-seat have flown.

Thither I fly, my God, my all,
To urge the one prevailing plea,
Which pardon and acceptance wins,
Thou, dearest Lord, hast died for me;

And now Thou livest evermore
To carry on Thy work of love,
And plead for us Thy precious death
In the eternal courts above.

O ever-living Sacrifice !
O Priest and Victim both in one !
Be Thou my Advocate, dear Lord,
Plead Thou my cause before the throne.

*JESU, GRANT ME POWER TO PLEAD.**

"Put me in remembrance: let us plead together: declare thou,
that thou mayest be justified."—*Isa.* xliii. 26.

JESU, grant me power to plead
For the pardon which I need;
Though my words be faint and dull,
Though my life of crime be full,
Though my soul be stained by sin,
Though my heart be foul within,
Hear me, Christ, in mercy hear,
To my prayer incline Thine ear.

Deeper, darker are the stains
On my soul than Magdalen's,

---

* This hymn is adapted from one of the Penitential Hymns
of S. John Damascen. For several of the lines I am indebted
to a fragment inserted in Dr. W. C. Taylor's *Historical Outline
of the Progress of Biblical Criticism and Succession of Sacred
Literature.*

When she brought the ointment sweet
Humbly to anoint Thy feet.
Thou, O Lord, didst pardon there,
Yielding to her humble prayer;
Hear me also, gracious Lord,
Pardon to my sins afford.

All my thoughts to Thee are known,
All my actions, every one;
All are noted in Thy scroll
Ere completed in my soul.
Free, oh, free me from the weight
Of the sins which now I hate!
Wash me, Saviour, in the flood
Of Thine own most precious blood.

White as snow the spirits shine,
Cleansèd in that stream divine;
Oh, that gift so full and free,
Gracious Saviour, grant to me!
All my words are poor and weak,
To obtain the grace I seek:
Jesu, teach me how to plead
For the pardon which I need.

CAPTIVITY AND FREEDOM.

"Bring my soul out of prison that I may praise Thy name."
Psalm cxlii. 7.

GREAT God, I come to Thee
Burdened with care,
Sin-stained and sorrowful;
Yet, Lord, I dare
Pour out my soul to Thee—
Tell Thee my prayer.

O God, most merciful,
Pardon my sin,
Black as the deepest
Hidden within;
For Thy Son's sake, who died
Pardon to win.

This is my only hope,
This my one plea:

Jesus, Incarnate God,
Died to save me,
Died from sin's slavery
To set me free.

Free to serve Thee, my God,
Till time is o'er,
And Thou dost call me forth,
Through death's dark door,
To dwell with Thee in light
For evermore.

DEEP CALLETH UNTO DEEP.

"Out of the depths have I cried unto Thee, O Lord."
Psalm cxxx. 1.

My God, my God, from depths of sin
  To depths of love I cry !
Let love prevail, and free my soul
  From all its misery.

My sins are countless as the sands
  Which bound the vast sea shore ;
Unpardoned, they must hide from me
  Thy presence evermore.

But mercy is with Thee, my God,
  And stedfast is Thy word—
Pardon to give to contrite hearts,
  Through Jesus Christ our Lord.

Through Him I come to Thee, my God ;
  His Blood is all my plea,
Full peace and pardon to effect
  Between my soul and Thee.

H

Oh, blessedness beyond all thought
· To taste the heavenly grace,
Which shows us, even upon earth,
    Thy reconcilèd face !

Which sweetly tells us we are Thine,
    In spite of all past sin,
And may, if faithful to the end,
    Our heavenly mansions win.

Make this grace fully mine, my Lord;
    To me, oh, let it be
A well of water springing up
    Into eternity !

OUR ONLY REFUGE IN TROUBLE.

"Mine eyes fail for Thy word, saying, When wilt Thou comfort
me?"—*Psalm* cxix. 82.

COMFORT me, O my God;
In mercy comfort me,
For sorrow and distress
Around my spirit press.
Oh, grant me sweet relief
From my heart-searching grief!
Comfort me, O my God;
In mercy comfort me.

The sins of all my life,
In all their dread array,
Now passed beyond control,
Are pressing down my soul.
Oh, free me from the weight
Of sins which now I hate!
Comfort me, O my God;
In mercy comfort me.

My sins deserve much more
Than all this chastisement.
I know it, O my God;
Yet turn away Thy rod,
Or, rather, give me grace
To see a Father's face,
Guiding, from heaven above,
Each pang in chastening love.

Into the vast abyss
Of Thine unbounded love,
Shown forth on Calvary
For sinners such as me,
I cast my sins, and cry,
With faith, and contrite sigh:
Comfort me, O my God;
In mercy comfort me.

OPEN-HEARTED PENITENCE.

"If we confess our sins, He is faithful and just to forgive us
our sins."—I *John* i. 9.

O GOD, my sorrows and my sins
    To Thee are fully known;
The inmost secrets of my soul
    Are bare to Thee alone.
I would not have it otherwise;
    I would not hide from Thee
The things on which one day must shine
    Light of eternity.

Though all to Thee are known, my God,
    Yet 'tis Thy will for me
That I, in sorrow, faith, and love,
    Should all confess to Thee;
And lay all bare my heart's desires,
    My trouble and my grief,
And seek of Thee, and Thee alone,
    True comfort and relief.

Therefore to Thee I now spread forth
    Griefs which my soul oppress,
As Hezekiah did of old,
    Seeking from Thee redress.
Oh, send some messenger of love,
    Who to my soul shall say,
" Fear not; in Me thou shalt find strength,
    However dark thy day !"

THE ALL PREVAILING PLEA.

"The Blood of Jesus Christ . . . cleanseth us from all sin."
1 *John* i. 7.

THE Blood of Christ is all my plea,
Father, when I draw nigh to Thee;
The Blood of Christ is all my plea
    Thy justice to appease.

Upon the Cross 'twas shed for me
To save my soul from misery;
Upon the Cross 'twas shed for me
    To cleanse me from my sin.

O Blood of Jesus, cleanse Thou me
From sin and its dread penalty;
O Blood of Jesus, cleanse Thou me
    From every guilty stain.

And when my pilgrimage is o'er,
Still let me know its saving power,
And find true peace in my last hour
    Through Christ's atoning Blood.

The Prayer of Faith.

" Whatsoever ye shall ask the Father in My Name, He will
give it you."—*S. John* xvi. 23.

JESU, as I gaze upon Thee,
   Lifted on the Cross of shame,
I would ask these great petitions
   Through the power of Thy great Name :

Break my heart with contrite sorrow
   For the sins I now bemoan,
And for which, in untold anguish,
   Thou, my Saviour, didst atone.

Give me Faith, that I may ever
   Fix my stedfast trust on Thee,
And o'ercome, in life's long battle,
   In the strength Thou givest me.

Give me Hope—the soul's great anchor
    In temptation's dangerous storm ;
On the surging, angry billows
    Let me see Thy living form.

Give me Love, my blessed Saviour,
    Who didst show such love for me
On the *Viâ Dolorosâ*,
    On the Cross of Calvary.

With these gifts no harm can touch me,
    As I tread the narrow way,
Leading through life's toils and sorrows
    To Thy home of endless day.

Vision of Jesus Crucified.

"Look unto Me, and be ye saved."—*Isa.* xlv. 22.

COME, my soul, in love adoring,
　View the ransom paid for thee;
Look on Jesus, bleeding, dying,
　On the Cross of Calvary.

Nearer draw, and gaze upon Him;
　Shrink not from the awful sight;
Do thy sins look black and many?
　Lo! His love is infinite.

Though thy sins be red like crimson,
　Numerous as the stars of heaven,
Through the cleansing Blood of Jesus
　All, yea, all may be forgiven.

All thy sins of early childhood,
　All thy sins of later years,
All the sins which stored in memory
　Fill thy soul with searching fears.

"Look on Me, and be ye savèd,"
　Hear Him saying from the Cross :
"Oh, miss not so great salvation !
　Count all other things as dross !

"Lay thy burden down before Me,
　With true faith and contrite grief ;
I can give thee rest and comfort,
　Peace and joy, and sweet relief."

Lord, I come ; Thy love hath drawn me ;
　Lord, I come to be forgiven ;
Lord, I come to ask for graces
　Which shall fit my soul for heaven.

Glory be to Thee, Lord Jesus,
　For Thy boundless love to me ;
Grant that I may know its fulness
　Through a blest eternity.

The First Words from the Cross.

"Father, forgive them; for they know not what they do."
S. Luke xxiii. 34.

LISTEN ! Lo ! the King of Sorrows,
From the Cross—His altar-throne,
Speaks to us in all the anguish
Which He bears for us alone.

See, the thorns His brow are piercing !
Nails now tear His hands and feet ;
What the first words which He utters,
His fierce murderers to greet ?

"Heavenly Father, oh, forgive them !
What they do they know not now ;
Let the Blood they shed plead for them,
From My feet, and hands, and brow.

"Look on ME, My heavenly Father,
Look on ME, not on their sin ;
See ME on the Cross extended,
Pardon e'en for them to win.

" And, O Father, through the ages,
　Even to the end of time,
Pardon grant to every sinner,
　Whatsoe'er may be his crime,

" Who shall seek for full forgiveness
　Through the sacramental tide,
Which flows forth, for their salvation,
　From My hands, and feet, and side."

Hear our Saviour, sinners, hear Him ;
　All-prevailing is His prayer ;
We may all obtain salvation
　If we to His Cross repair,

If, before Him meekly kneeling,
　In repentance, faith, and love,
We accept the full salvation
　Which He offers from above.

Draw us, heavenly Father ; draw us
　Through all earthly care and loss
To seek mercy, peace, and pardon
　Through Thy Son upon the Cross.

Evening of Good Friday.

ALL along the blood-stained way,
Leading to Mount Calvary's height,
We have followed Thee, dear Lord,
From first dawn to gathering night.

All Thy sorrow, grief, and shame—
More than human words can say—
Which Thou didst for us endure,
We have pondered o'er to-day.

We have seen Thee raised on high,
Nailèd to the destined tree;
And for three long hours have watched
All Thy dying agony.

Now the solemn day is past,
Which Thy Church has set apart
For each faithful child to learn
All Thy sufferings, Lord, by heart.

Oh, by all Thou didst endure—
Shame and anguish, grief and pain—
Grant that we may never more
Crucify Thee, Lord, again !

But in mercy give us grace
So to measure all Thy love,
That our hearts may evermore
Be with Thee in Heaven above.

Easter Day.

" This is the day which the Lord hath made ; we will rejoice
and be glad in it."—*Psalm* cxviii. 24.

Ye chosen servants of the King of kings,
His praises sing to-day with glad acclaim,
Join in the anthems which Christ's Holy Church
Chants forth in honour of His glorious Name ;
Now with fresh hope may we pursue our way,
For Christ hath risen from the dead to-day.

Oh, tell it out amongst the heathen lands
That Christ, the Virgin's Son, is Lord of all !
Let the glad sound go forth, that all may learn
Upon Messiah's saving Name to call,
And with us gladly tread our heavenward way,
For Christ hath risen from the dead to-day.

Hail, Holy Jesus, Victor over death !
   Hail, mighty Saviour, all Thy pains are o'er !
Thine is the kingdom, Thine the glory now,
   Crushed is the serpent's head for evermore ;
Therefore with hope we tread our heavenward way,
   For Thou hast risen from the dead to-day.

Saviour, be with us as we journey on
   Through this strange country to our home with Thee,
That, dying daily to all sinful ways,
   We may rise daily to life new and free,
And with fresh hope pursue our heavenward way,
   Since Thou hast risen from the dead to-day.

And when at last through Jordan we must pass,
   Oh, may we see Thy face on Canaan's strand
Ready to greet us with Thy loving smile,
   And lead us onward to the promised land !
There with Thee, risen Saviour, to abide,
   Tasting the joys of heavenly Eastertide.

114

Ascension.

THE KING'S RETURN.

"Lift up your heads, O ye gates; and be ye lift up, ye everlasting doors; and the King of Glory shall come in."—*Psalm* xxiv. 7.

RING out your Alleluias,
    Ye heavenly choirs on high!
To His bright realm of glory
    Your King is drawing nigh.
His earthly pains are over,
    Redemption's work is done;
Sing of the great salvation
    Which our great Chief hath won.

Worship your God Incarnate,
    The blessed Virgin's Son,
Who is with God the Father
    And God the Spirit One.

Sing the new song, ye blest ones :
" Worthy the Lamb once slain,
To take all power and glory
   On Heaven's high throne again."

Shall we not, ransomed Christians,
   Our voices also raise
To swell the mighty chorus
   Of our Redeemer's praise?
Shall we not sing with gladness
   Of Christ's redeeming love?
And join the heavenly concert
   Which welcomes Him above?

We greet Thee, conquering Saviour,
   On this high festal day,
When Thou from earth to Heaven
   Didst tread thy glorious way.
May we with Thee, dear Jesus,
   In heart and mind ascend,
And dwell with Thee in glory
   Through ages without end.

THE HEAVENWARD GAZERS.

"Why stand ye gazing up into heaven?"—*Acts* i. 11.

WHY stand ye gazing thus into the heaven,
Apostles true of your ascended Lord,
Ye who have loved and followed Him so long,
And lived upon His every act and word?

Ye cannot follow now your risen Lord,
Or join the ranks of that angelic train,
Which welcomes Him, their everlasting King,
Back to His throne in highest heaven again.

Ye cannot follow now, but in calm trust
Ye must your Sovereign's royal will obey,
And others train to love and follow Him
Into the regions of eternal day.

Suff'ring and sorrow, shame and grief and pain,
Must be your portion for a little space,
Then shall ye follow with a ransomed throng,
To whom ye have made known Christ's saving grace.

Oh, better then than now, when your deep love
Has been well tested in pain's cleansing fire !
When ye have laboured, witnessed, suffered, died,
For Him, your Love, your Joy, your Heart's Desire.

Then shall ye follow your ascended Lord,
Then, when your glorious work on earth is o'er,
Then, with a countless host, fruits of His death,
Shall ye rejoin your Lord for evermore.

THE KING'S TRIUMPH.

"Thou hast ascended on high, Thou hast led captivity captive.'
Psalm lxviii. 18.

JESUS, our Lord, hath triumphed;
He hath gone up on high,
To live and reign in glory
Throughout eternity;
To claim the ceaseless worship
Of all the heavenly host,
With God the Almighty Father,
And God the Holy Ghost.

Jesus, our Lord, hath triumphed;
His sufferings now are o'er;
Though He once died in weakness,
He reigneth now in power.
No words can tell His glory,
Who once towards Calvary trod
To die for guilty sinners,
And win them back to God.

Jesus, our Lord, hath triumphed;
But we, in toil and pain,
Must fight our life-long battle
Until He comes again;
Fight, in His help depending,
To aid us in the strife,
And bring us through all dangers
To everlasting life.

Jesus, our Lord, hath triumphed;
In Him we triumph too:
If in our daily conflict
We strive His will to do,
And fix our hearts' affections
On His unchanging love,
Then shall we share His triumph
In His bright realms above.

The King Reigning on High.

" Thine eyes shall see the King in His beauty: they shall behold
the land which is very far off."—*Isaiah* xxxiii. 17.

THE King in His beauty is reigning on high,
On the throne of His glory beyond the blue sky;
No words we can utter can ever declare
The vision of rapture He manifests there.
Lord Jesu, sweet Saviour, sole Fountain of grace,
Oh, grant us the joy of beholding Thy face !

All the bright things of earth which around us we view
Are but emblems and pictures of beauties more true,
Which, in their full glory and splendour divine,
In that heavenly country eternally shine.
Lord Jesu, sweet Saviour, sole Fountain of grace,
Oh, grant us the joy of beholding Thy face !

All the sweet sounds of music and heart-thrilling song,
Which solace us here as we journey along,
What are these to the anthems which angels there sing,
To God their Creator, Preserver, and King ?

Lord Jesu, sweet Saviour, sole Fountain of grace,
Oh, grant us the joy of beholding Thy face !

Very far, far away is that region of light—
That fair land of beauty and endless delight ;
Yet the keen eye of faith can o'erspan the abyss,
And fix the soul's hope on her infinite bliss.
Lord Jesu, sweet Saviour, sole Fountain of grace,
Oh, grant us the joy of beholding Thy face !

Fight bravely the battle ; contend for the crown,
The kingdom of glory, the endless renown,
The rapture of hearing our King speak the word,
" True servant, inherit the joy of thy Lord."
Lord Jesu, sweet Saviour, sole Fountain of grace,
Oh, grant us the joy of beholding Thy face !

Press onward, press onward, it will not be long,
Ere we join in the chorus of heavenly song ;
Ere to all things of this world we whisper adieu,
And the King in His beauty breaks forth to our view.
Lord Jesu, sweet Saviour, sole Fountain of grace,
Oh, grant us the joy of beholding Thy face !

Our Ever-Living Advocate.

"We have an Advocate with the Father."—1 *John* ii. 1.

I HAVE an Advocate on high,
Who pleads for me both night and day ;
I need not perish in my sins,
For Jesus is the sinner's stay.

He died upon the cross for me,
Paying in full redemption's price ;
Off'ring Himself, both God and man,
Our all-sufficient Sacrifice.

And still that Sacrifice He pleads
Before the Father's throne in heaven,
As the one ground why guilty man
May claim to have his sins forgiven.

And He has given us a way
His all-prevailing death to show,
In sacramental mystery,
In His most Holy Church below.

Oft as the vested priest draws nigh,
Before the altar high to stand,
Bringing forth gifts of bread and wine,
As Christ our Saviour gave command,

And there enacts the solemn rite,
And speaks the words by Jesus given—
Then is the worship here on earth
One with the worship paid in heaven.

Jesus, and Jesus crucified—
In heaven and earth this is the plea
Which can bring pardon, peace, and joy
To all, my God, who come to Thee.

And this shall be my only plea
Through life, and with my latest breath;
Oh, may I know its saving power,
Both now and in the hour of death!

I have an Advocate on high,
His prayers with mine for ever blend;
I need not perish in my sins,
For Jesus is the sinner's friend.

Charitas Christi Urget Nos.

"The love of Christ constraineth us."—2 *Cor.* v. 14.

Servant of God, midst toil and strife,
Midst worldly sorrow, pain, or loss,
Let this your watchword be through life,
"*Charitas Christi urget nos.*"

When the world seeks with glittering scenes
To lure thee from thy Saviour's cross,
Oh, let these words recall thy soul,
"*Charitas Christi urget nos.*"

When sinful passion surges high,
Oh, take heed lest ye suffer loss!
Still the wild tumult with the words,
"*Charitas Christi urget nos.*"

When sinful thoughts, impure or vain,
Flit like black clouds thy soul across,
Disperse them with the inspiring words,
"*Charitas Christi urget nos.*"

When faith seems dull, and love grows cold,
And hard to thee appears thy cross,
Think of thy Saviour's love, and say,
"*Charitas Christi urget nos.*"

The toil is brief, endless the joy,
Oh, sell it not for earthly dross!
Press bravely onward to the end,
"*Charitas Christi urget nos.*"

This—this can ever stay the soul
In deadly pain or crushing loss,
And bear thee safely to the goal—
"*Charitas Christi urget nos.*"

Oh, love of Jesus, urge us on,
Gladly to bear our daily cross!
Whate'er betide be this our guide,
"*Charitas Christi urget nos.*"

Jesus, Meek and Gentle.*

Jesus, meek and gentle,
Son of God Most High,
Pitying, loving Saviour,
Hear Thy children's cry.

Pardon our offences ;
Loose our captive chains ;
Break down every idol
Which our soul detains.

Give us holy freedom ;
Fill our hearts with love ;
Draw us, Holy Jesus,
To the realms above.

---

* This little hymn has found its way into most English Hymn
Books. It is commonly thought to have been written for
children, and on this supposition I have been asked to simplify
the fourth verse. The hymn was not, however, written
specially for children. Where it is used in collections of
hymns for children, it might be well to alter the two last
lines in the fourth verse thus—

"Through earth's passing darkness,
To heaven's endless day."

Lead us on our journey ;
    Be Thyself the Way
Through terrestrial darkness
    To celestial day.

Jesus, meek and gentle,
    Son of God Most High,
Pitying, loving Saviour,
    Hear Thy children's cry.

Thanksgiving Hymn.

"I will praise Thee with my whole heart."—*Psalm* cxxxviii. 1.

O JESUS, merciful and true,
    My only Lord and King,
To Thee my love and thanks are due ;
    Thy praises will I sing.

I praise Thee for the boundless love
    Which brought Thee down from heaven
To labour, agonize, and die,
    That I might be forgiven.

I praise Thee for that cleansing grace,
 The virtue of Thy Blood,
Which washed my soul from nature's sin
 In the baptismal flood.

I praise Thee for the tender care
 Shed o'er my early youth,
Which led me in the Church's way
 Of holiness and truth.

I praise Thee for the gift of gifts,
 In deepest mystery given—
Thyself, our sacramental food,
 The living Bread from heaven.

I thank Thee, Lord, for all the gifts
 Stored in Thy Church for me,
To strengthen me through life's long day,
 And fit my soul for Thee.

Uía Crucis, Uía Lucis.

" If we suffer, we shall also reign with Him."
2 *Tim*. ii. 12.

WOULDST thou enjoy the eternal years
With Christ beyond the shining spheres?
Count well the cost—nor think to gain
That bliss without a passing pain.

For thee Thy Lord bore heaven's loss;
For thee endured the painful Cross;
Scorn, pain, and agonizing throe,
To save thee from eternal woe.

And 'tis thy gracious Father's will
That all His heavenly courts who fill,
Should suffer now for Jesus' sake,
Ere they His endless bliss partake.

Look well, then, on thy suffering Lord;
Study His every act and word;
Take up thy cross with reverent care,
In meekness after Him to bear.

K

Keen though the sorrow, sharp the grief,
Jesus can give thee sweet relief,
And cleanse thy soul from earthly dross,
Beneath the shadow of His Cross.

Yea, Jesu, every pang shall be
But light which we can bear for Thee;
Our keenest woe to joy shall turn,
If Thy blest love within us burn.

To God the Father, God the Son,
And God the Spirit, Three in One,
Be praise and adoration given,
By all on earth and all in heaven.

The True Haven.

"So He bringeth them unto their desired haven."
Psalm cvii. 30.

Jesu, dearest Saviour,
    Through life's stormy sea
Bring us to the haven
    Where our souls would be.

Let not sin or sorrow
    Draw us from Thy side;
They alone dwell safely
    Who with Thee abide.

Many foes surround us,
    Many dwell within;
By Thy mighty power
    Save us, Lord, from sin.

Satan and his angels
    Tempt us every hour;
We can foil the tempter
    Only in Thy power.

Oh, then, Jesu, Saviour,
　Never let us roam
From Thy sheltering guidance
　Till we reach our home !

Home !　O word of rapture !
　Evermore with Thee
In the heavenly Salem,
　By the crystal sea,

Joining in the anthem
　Which through Heaven shall ring :
Holy, holy, holy,
　To our God and King.

Onward through the ages,
　Which shall never end,
We would our weak voices
　With these praises blend.

Agnus Dei.

O LORD JESUS ! Lamb of God !
We will sing Thy praises :
Thou canst save us from our sins,
Thou canst give us graces ;
Thou canst guard us all through life,
Though fierce Satan rageth ;
Thy word stills the stormy blast,
And its waves assuageth.

O sweet Jesus ! Lamb of God !
By the red blood streaming
From Thy hands and wounded side
For the world's redeeming,
Wash my soul from every stain
In that wondrous river,
Which from Thee, true Rock, doth flow,
My soul to deliver.

O Lord Jesus ! Lamb of God !
Thou wast pure and holy,
Merciful and kind and good,
Loving, meek, and lowly ;
Thou dost bid us gaze on Thee,
And Thy footsteps follow,
Looking through life's toilsome day
For a bright to-morrow.

Yet the way seems long, O Lord,
Very sad and dreary ;
Sin surrounds me, and ofttime
I am very weary.
But, dear Jesus, speak to me,
In my hours of sadness,
Words which kindle love, and turn
Sorrow into gladness.

Jesus ! living Lamb of God !
In that home of glory
Which Thou hast made known to us
In the Gospel story,

There are lamb-like virgin souls,
  Which, dear Lord, Thou knowest,
Who in rapture follow Thee
  Wheresoe'er Thou goest.

Holy Jesus! Lamb of God!
  Look on us with pity;
Through Thy mercy we are heirs
  Of that heavenly city;
We are lambs of Thine own flock,
  Oh, let nothing sever
That sweet bond which makes us Thine
  For ever and for ever!

Loving Trust.

"Blessed is the man that trusteth in Thee."
Psalm lxxxiv. 12.

MERCIFUL Jesus, give us grace
 To fix our trust in Thee ;
For those alone who trust Thee well
 Can know true liberty.

When pain of body lays us low,
 Then may we trust Thee still
To give us ease or strengthen us,
 As Thou, dear Lord, shalt will.

When keenest sorrow fills our hearts
 For loved ones passed away,
O loving Saviour, give us strength
 According to our day !

In want, may we still trust Thee, Lord ;
 All riches are Thine own ;
But poverty may be the way
 To lead us to Thy throne.

And should disgrace or shame be ours,
   In calm trust may we say,
Lord, we but share what Thou didst bear
   Along the dolorous way.

Thus may we ever trust Thee, Lord,
   In sorrow, pain, or shame;
And only strive to do Thy will,
   And glorify Thy name.

In Bodily Pain.

JESUS Christ, my only Saviour,
  In my grief I fly to Thee ;
Thou art merciful and mighty,
  In Thy mercy look on me.

I can bear my pain, dear Jesus,
  If it be Thy holy will ;
But I need Thy grace to help me
  All Thy wishes to fulfil.

Give me loving trust and patience,
  Give me grace Thy form to see
Walking round me, gazing on me,
  In my pain and agony.

All will then be well, dear Jesus,
  Whatsoe'er my pains may be ;
Blessèd are they if they only
  Knit me closer, Lord, to Thee.

Hymn of the Evening Light.

JOYFUL Light of God the Father,
　Jesus, Everlasting Son,
Laud and praise to Thee we offer
　As sinks down yon glorious sun.

As the shadows close around us,
　Sun of Righteousness, true Light,
Fill our spirits with Thy brightness
　Through the silent hours of night.

Tune our hearts to sing Thy praises,
　Thou who through the toilsome day
Hast been ever, to Thy chosen,
　Light, and Life, and Living Way.

Grant us, through the hours of darkness,
　Rest from care, and toil, and sin,
Rest from fierce temptation's power,
　Peace without, and peace within.

And when life's long day is ended,
　Light of Light, illume our way
Through the vale of death's deep shadows
　To Thy home of endless day.

Thanksgiving for Church Blessings.

"The Church of God, which He hath purchased with His own Blood."—*Acts* xx. 28.

Upon the painful Cross of shame
God bought His Church with His own Blood,
And set her up, like Beacon bright,
To draw men to that cleansing Flood.

We bless Thy holy Name, O Lord,
For placing us Thy Church within,
And by Thy free baptismal grace
Cleansing our souls from nature's sin.

We bless Thee for the heavenly Food
Which, in the riches of Thy love,
Thou hast provided for our souls—
Thyself, true Manna from above.

Oh, loving Saviour, grant that we
May live and die within Thy Fold,
And then to Paradise be led,
Thy glorious presence to behold!

To taste that living spring of joy,
Welling from out Thy radiant throne,
Unfailing, pure, without alloy,
Which freely Thou dost give Thine own.

Lord, may Thy Church her charge fulfil,
And spread Thy truth from pole to pole,
Preaching release to captive hearts,
Since Thou hast ransomed every soul.

To Thee, O blessèd Trinity,
Let praises evermore be given,
By all Thy servants here on earth,
And all the denizens of heaven.

The Church's Final Victory.

"Awake, awake; put on thy strength, O Zion."—*Isa.* lii. 1.

CHURCH of the living God, arise,
Gird on thy strength as in past days;
Faint not, and fear not, God is strong;
His strength is thine in all thy ways.

What though thy foes are fierce and bold,
Is not thy Saviour's promise sure—
"Lo! I am with you to the end,
Long as the days of time endure"?

The wrath of man, and Satan's hosts,
May join thy bulwarks to assail;
Vainly they beat against thy walls:
"The Church of Christ can never fail."

Built on the everlasting Rock;
Calmly on Christ she stands secure,
Around her kingdoms rise and fall;
'Tis hers for ever to endure.

Church of the living God, arise,
Draw the eternal Spirit's sword ;
Smite down God's enemies, and thine,
Through Jesus Christ, the Incarnate Word.

The victory must be Thine at last ;
Error must perish, truth must reign.
Oh, may we share Thy triumph-day,
When Christ, our Saviour, comes again !

The Bride's Jewels.

"Prepared as a Bride adorned for her Husband."
Rev. xxi. 2.

THE Bride of Christ adornèd stands,
With many a jewel bright,
Culled from all ages and all lands
To be her Lord's delight.
Saints glitter in her coronet
Of many a varied hue;
In purest gold the gems are set,
And shine with lustre true.

O King of saints, to us impart
Such grace as Thou dost see
Will aid us to obtain a place
Midst this blest company!

Rubies tell of the martyr band,
Who through the sea of blood,
Reached Jesus and the happy land
Beyond death's gathering flood.

Of confessors the diamond speaks,
  Shining with radiance bright,
And showing, to each soul that seeks,
  Rays from the one true Light.
    O King of saints, to us impart, &c.

The pearl, with quiet lustre, shows
  The depth of that pure love,
Which in the Virgin's spirit glows
  For her dear Spouse above.
The emerald, with hue of earth,
  Yet free from all alloy,
Tells of the hidden saints whose worth
  Shall gain eternal joy.
    O King of saints, to us impart, &c.

The amethyst, with purple rays,
  Speaks of that lowly train,
Who through true penitential ways
  Their birthright did regain.
The jasper and the onyx stone,
  The yellow topaz clear,
Like varied saints, in this are one,
  They all to Christ are dear.
    O King of saints, to us impart, &c.

L

These all adorn Christ's chosen Bride,
They shine for Christ her King ;
To His dear love, and nought beside,
They owe their glistering.
Right precious in their Saviour's sight
Are all these souls elect,
Which deck His Bride in glory bright,
And grace her coronet.

O King of saints, to us impart
Such grace as Thou dost see
Will aid us to obtain a place
Midst this blest company !

Feast of the Annunciation.

"And the angel came in unto her, and said, Hail, thou that art highly favoured, the Lord is with thee : blessed art thou among women."—*S. Luke* i. 28.

SING to-day with holy joy
    And exultant gladness;
Lo! an angel comes from heaven
    To dispel our sadness.

Whither hies the Spirit blest?
    To a Virgin holy,
In sweet converse with her God,
    In her chamber lowly.

What the message which from heaven
    Gabriel is laden,
As he hovers round the shrine
    Of the saintly maiden?

" Hail ! choice vessel, full of grace ;
Hail ! blest Virgin, holy ;
God in heaven loves to dwell
With the meek and lowly.

" Favour thou hast found with God,
Before every other,
Of the Saviour of the world
To become the Mother."

Meekly kneels the Virgin blest,
Her sweet spirit bending
To God's will in glad consent,
To our joy unending.

Praise we then our God to-day
For Christ's incarnation,
Which through Mary, brought to man
Pardon and salvation.

Nativity of the Blessed Virgin Mary.

"In that day will I cause the horn of the house of Israel
to bud forth."—*Ezekiel* xxix. 21.

VISION of purity and love divine,
How, through all ages, doth thy glory shine !
Chosen of God from all eternity
The mother of His only Son to be.
Oh, joyous day, when Anna gave thee birth,
Elected shrine of God upon this earth !

Thy God hath magnified thee, holy Maid ;
The glory which He gives can never fade :
Nations of every language, race, and clime,
Shall call thee blessèd to the end of time.
Oh, joyous day, when Anna gave thee birth,
Elected shrine of God upon this earth !

Ah ! would we reach thy Son's bright home of day,
When this short life on earth has passed away,
We must, through His almighty grace so free,
Like thee, blest Mary, pure and humble be.
Oh, joyous day, when Anna gave thee birth,
Elected shrine of God upon this earth !

S. John Baptist.

"The voice of one crying in the wilderness, Prepare ye the
way of the Lord, make His paths straight."
S. Mark i. 3.

SAINTLY forerunner of the King of Saints,
Herald, Messiah's kingdom to proclaim,
Greatest of prophets, to the end of time
Honoured within the Church will be thy name.

Still rings thy thrilling voice, like clarion shrill,
Calling to sinners, in salvation's day,
"Repent; for soon your Lord will come again
In this world's desert—make for Him a way!"

Break down your haughty thoughts, your wayward wills;
Subdue them, till they bend beneath His sway:
Thus shall ye best prepare your King to meet,
When next He comes in glorious majesty.

Merciful Lord, let us not hear in vain
The voice which calls us to repentance meet;
Oh, give us grace to come with contrite hearts
And lay our sins and follies at Thy feet!

Then may we gaze upon the Lamb of God,
And in that vision find true joy and peace,
Since He has come to take our sins away,
And give us absolution and release.

152

S. Peter.

I.

"Thou art the Christ, the Son of the living God. . . Blessed
art thou, Simon Barjona."—*S. Matt.* xvii. 16, 17.

PRINCE and Apostle in the Church of God,
First of the chosen twelve, by Christ's decree,
First, with true faith and courage to confess
The saving truth of His Divinity.

"Blest art thou, Simon," spake the eternal Word ;
"For unto thee my Father hath made known
The truth on which my Church shall now be built,
That I am Christ, the living Father's Son.

"Against this Church not all the powers of hell
Shall ever to the end of time prevail ;
Take this my promise as your sure defence,
When deadly enemies that Church assail."

We claim Thy promise, Lord ; for round Thy Church
Thy foes are gathering with discordant sound.
They gaze on Her with scorn, as erst on Thee,
And cry, " Down with Her, even to the ground."

Come to our aid in this our hour of need ;
Come, mighty Saviour, speak Thy word of power ;
Scatter Thine enemies, and let Thy Church
Find strength in Thee in every trying hour.

And give us grace, like Peter, to confess
The one true faith before a faithless world,
Nor shrink truth's holy warfare to maintain,
Where'er its sacred banner is unfurled.

S. PETER.

II.

"The Lord turned, and looked upon Peter."—*S. Luke* xxii. 61.
"Simon, son of Jonas, lovest thou Me?"—*S. John* xxi. 15.

NOBLE Confessor of the faith,
We hail thee on thy festal day;
On thy confession, as a Rock,
The Church will stand secure for aye.

Though for a moment thou didst fail,
One look from Christ, one silent call,
Plunged thee in penitential tears,
And wrought repentance for thy fall.

Yet ere the Searcher of all hearts
Gifted thee with the pastor's part,
And bade thee feed His purchased flock,
Deeply He tried thy loving heart.

"Lovest thou Me? Though firm thy faith,
True pastors must be loving too;
For nought but love can nerve their souls
For the great work they have to do."

Well didst thou stand the test, blest saint ;
For love burnt brightly in thy soul ;
Ready wert thou to live and die
For Christ, thy King, thy God, thy All.

O Lord, endue Thy pastors still
With faith and love, Thy gifts Divine,
That they may guard and feed Thy flock,
And keep them ever truly Thine,

Until the day when, round Thy throne,
Pastors and sheep alike shall stand,
Ever to love and worship Thee
In heaven's true fold, our native land.

SS. Peter and Andrew.

"Jesus, walking by the sea of Galilee, saw two brethren, Simon called Peter, and Andrew his brother. . He saith unto them, Follow Me."—*S. Matt.* iv. 18, 19.

As walked the Saviour of the world
Beside the Galilean sea,
He saw two brothers at their toil,
And simply uttered, "Follow Me."

The words fell on their souls with power,
And moved them to obey the call;
At once they left their boats and nets,
For Jesus' sake forsaking all.

How often hast Thou called us, Lord,
In words of tenderness and love,
Bidding us quit some earthly cares,
To gain from Thee gifts from above.

And oh ! alas ! how oft have we
Refused to heed Thy loving voice,
And fondly clung to earthly things,
Making them, and not Thee, our choice.

Oh, call us yet again, dear Lord,
And from vain cares our hearts set free,
That we may heed Thy loving call,
And through life's journey follow Thee !

S. James, Apostle and Martyr.

"Jesus said unto them, Ye shall indeed drink of the cup that I drink of; and with the baptism that I am baptized withal shall ye be baptized."—*S. Mark* x. 38.

.

FOLLOW now your blessèd Lord,
Holy James, apostle true ;
Freely give your life to Him
Who His life-blood gave for you.

Lo ! He calls you forth to-day
To the baptism of blood ;
Meekly, bravely bathe your soul
In that sacramental flood.

Blessèd lot, with Him to share
In His cup of pain and woe ;
Blessèd in His strength to gain
Victory o'er every foe.

Blessèd then, behind the veil,
Thy beloved Lord to meet,
Waiting thee, His martyr blest,
With His welcome smile to greet.

Now thou reignest with thy Lord;
Crownèd is thy noble brow;
For, blest martyr, through His strength,
More than conqueror wert thou.

King of martyrs, give us grace
Gentle, true, and brave to be,
When thou callest us to share
Earthly suffering, Lord, for Thee.

And when, through the gate of death,
We must pass to scenes unknown,
Let us not, O Shepherd true,
Tread the shadowy path alone.

But be near us in that hour,
Guide us with Thy staff and rod,
As our souls these bodies leave,
To present themselves to God.

S. Matthew.

"Jesus saw a man, named Matthew, sitting at the receipt of custom : and He saith unto him, Follow Me.　And he arose, and followed Him."—*S. Matt.* ix. 9.

O LORD, how truly blest are they
Who, drawn by Thy attracting love,
Have grace to leave their earthly things
For the true riches stored above.

S. Matthew won that special grace
When, in response to Thy blest call,
He left his place of earthly gain,
Freely for Thee forsaking all.

He heard Thy summons, " Follow Me,"
And quickly hastened to obey ;
He cherished Thy electing love,
Nor wasted it by sad delay.

He followed Thee, His well-loved Lord,
Throughout Thy life of grief and pain ;
Enduring treasures now are his,
And Thy loved face he sees again.

Like Thy Apostle, Lord, may we
On heavenly treasures fix our choice,
And quickly rise and follow Thee
Whene'er we hear Thy loving voice.

That, passing through earth's toils and cares,
With our affections fixed on Thee,
Thou mayest, Lord, our great Reward
And everlasting Portion be.

Jesus, we praise Thee for the grace
To Thine elect Apostle given ;
May we, like him, true riches gain,
And praise Thee evermore in heaven.

162

Saints' Days.

CHRIST GLORIFIED IN HIS SAINTS.

"Glorified in His saints . . . admired in all them that believe."
2 *Thess.* i. 10.

Hail, holy Jesus, King of saints !
The glory of the saints is Thine ;
The gems of grace which deck their souls,
Through Thee, true Light, so brightly shine.

We glorify Thee in Thy saints ;
For, Lord, it was Thy holy will
To form in them Thine image pure,
And with Thy love their spirits fill.

Their holiness was all from Thee ;
From Thee their faith and hope and love ;
Through suffering here, they followed Thee
To Thine eternal throne above.

Lord, give us grace to follow them,
As they in patience followed Thee,
That with them we may taste the joy
Of seeing Thee eternally.

To Father, Son, and Holy Ghost
Be praise and adoration given,
By saints below and saints above,
And all the angelic host in heaven.

THE BEAUTY OF HOLINESS.

" All Thy works shall praise Thee, O Lord ; and Thy saints
shall bless Thee."—*Psalm* cxlv. 10.

LOVELY are all Thy works, O God,
    In earth, and sea, and sky ;
They join in showing forth Thy praise
    And glorious majesty.

Yet lovelier still Thy works of grace,
    Our ransomed souls within,
Cleansing us with Thy precious blood
    From guilty stains of sin.

Endowing us with heavenly gifts,
    Wrought by Thy Spirit's might ;
Fitting our souls to dwell with Thee
    In everlasting light.

Lord, in us carry on Thy work,
   Till we that land attain
Where never more, in thought or deed,
   Our spirits we can stain.

Where saints and angels round Thy throne
   Pour forth in ceaseless lays,
To Father, Son, and Holy Ghost,
   Their anthems of high praise.

Lovely are all Thy works, O God;
   But loveliest, souls that shine
Resplendent in Thy righteousness,
   Jesu, true Sun Divine.

THE HEIRS OF THE KINGDOM.

"The saints of the Most High shall take the kingdom, and
possess the kingdom for ever, even for ever and ever."
Daniel vii. 18.

BLESSÈD are all Thy saints, O Lord,
Whate'er the path they trod,
Which led them through all earthly things,
To Thee, the living God.

Some heard Thy call in early youth,
And hastened to obey,
Following through life Thy blessèd steps,
Along the narrow way.

And some received Thy saving call
In life's maturer years,
And gladdened angels with their sighs
And penitential tears.

O Lord, Thy grace worked mightily
In all these souls elect,
And strengthened them at last to win
Their heavenly coronet.

In our souls also, gracious Lord,
May saving grace abound,
That with Thee, and Thy blessèd saints,
We may at last be found;

And taste the joys at Thy right hand,
The pleasures evermore,
Which for all saints and penitents
Thou hast, dear Lord, in store.

Martyrs.

"If we suffer, we shall also reign with Him."—2 *Tim.* ii. 12.

STAMPED with the royal sign
Of suffering, shame, and pain,
The meek Confessor stands
Before his judge again;
Again unmoved to see
The hard, unpitying frown,
And hear the words pronounced
Which give the martyr's crown.

Who amidst all the throng
Is now so bright as he,
As he goes forth to meet
His death of agony?
His pains will soon be o'er;
His last great fight is nigh :
Calmly he marches on
To glorious victory.

The Lord, upon His throne,
Is ever in his sight ;
The vision fills his soul
With rapturous delight.
" For ever with the Lord !"
That is the one desire
Which thrills his inmost soul
With its consuming fire.

Lord Jesus, as on Thee
The martyrs fixed their eyes,
When Thou didst call them forth
To win their glorious prize,
So, Lord, like them may we,
In all our daily strife,
Fix our souls' gaze on Thee,
The Way, the Truth, the Life.

Virgin Martyr.

"My Beloved is mine, and I am His."
Canticles ii. 16.

THE Maiden stands forth, in her virginal might,
For Christ and His honour to wage the great fight;
For Him she has lived, for Him she dares die;
In this her last struggle she knows He is nigh.

Though feeble and weak, yet her spirit is strong,
She fears not the rough men who bear her along;
She lifts up a prayer to Christ on His throne,
To grant them His pardon, and make them His own.

A vision of beauty lights up her bright eye;
Her heart is with Jesus beyond the blue sky;
Her Lord, her dear Lord, is in love looking down,
To see His brave Martyr contend for her crown.

All radiant with joy, she can bear every pain,
And count all as nothing, her loved One to gain ;
Like sunshine, His look illumines her soul,
Her Saviour, her Bridegroom, her God, and her All.

O Jesu, dear Lord, midst the toil and the strife
Which encompass our souls as we journey through life,
May we, like Thy martyrs in ages of old,
For Thee and Thy honour be steadfast and bold.

ffoteign fHissions.

GOSPEL MESSENGERS.

" How beautiful upon the mountains are the feet of him that
bringeth good tidings, that publisheth peace; that bringeth
good tidings of good, that publisheth salvation."

Isaiah lii. 7.

How blessèd are Thy servants, Lord,
Who, gifted with love's heavenly flame,
Go forth to distant heathen lands,
Thy glorious Gospel to proclaim !

Choice words of mercy, truth, and love
Fall from their lips, like gracious dew,
Softening the souls, fruitless and bare,
Until in Jesus Christ made new.

Great is their burden ; but, dear Lord,
How great the joy they find in Thee,
When they loose souls from Satan's chains,
And make them for Thy service free.

In toil, O Lord, be Thou their rest,
  Their sure defence in danger's hour,
May they their warfare well maintain,
  Strengthened by Thy almighty power.

And when their work on earth is done,
  And they their souls to Thee resign,
May they, around Thy throne on high,
  Like stars for ever brightly shine.

CHRIST'S CHOSEN HERALDS.

"Tell it out among the heathen that the Lord is King."
Psalm xcvi. 10.

YE chosen Heralds of the Lord,
  Go forth His message to proclaim !
Oh, tell to all the nations round
  The saving power of Jesus' name !

Tell them of Jesus' love for man,
  And tell them of His wondrous birth ;
Tell them He is Almighty God,
  Though as a man He lived on earth.

Tell them how every living soul
  May win salvation full and free,
If they will trust in Jesus Christ,
  And His obedient servants be.

Tell them of all the gifts of grace,
  Rich treasures of God's boundless love,
Stored in the Church for pilgrims true,
  Wending their way to heaven above.

Tell them of all which Christ hath done,
  Of all that He is doing now,
Until, filled with adoring love,
  Before the one true God they bow.

Ye chosen Heralds of the Lord,
  Go forth on your great work of love,
To share Christ's thorny crown below,
  And win a glorious crown above !

"*TOIL ON, BRAVE HEARTS.*"

" The ship was now in the midst of the sea, tossed with waves :
for the wind was contrary."—*S. Matt.* xiv. 24.

TOIL on, brave hearts ; toil on, dimly as yet
Can ye the distant longed-for haven see ;
Strong blows the adverse wind, therefore row well
If ye would reach the land where ye would be.

Toil on through weary hours ; He sent you forth
Whose holy will ye must for aye obey.
Trust in that mighty Saviour's power and love
To aid and strengthen you upon your way.

The night draws on, slowly the watches pass ;
If in your danger Jesus seems not nigh,
Yet struggle on, trust in His promise sure,
To hear His servants when to Him they cry.

Pray well in all your trials and your toils,
On Jesus let your faithful hearts be stayed ;
And ye in faith shall see your Lord draw nigh,
And hear Him say, " 'Tis I, be not afraid."

Home Missions.

"Seek ye the Lord while He may be found, call ye upon Him while He is near."—*Isaiah* lv. 6.

SINNER, quickly seek thy Saviour,
Seek thy Saviour dear;
    Time is hurrying fast away,
    Make no more delay.

Think how often Christ has called thee
From the ways of sin;
    Waiting long to bring thee back
    To the heavenward track.

Spurn no more His voice so loving,
Spurn no more His voice;
    If ye heed His accents blest,
    He will give you rest,—

Rest from sin and sin's hard bondage,
Rest from deadly sin.
  Oh, lose not the blissful peace
  Of that sweet release!

Oh, return! for life is flying,
Flying fast away.
  Soon will action, voice, and breath
  All be stilled in death.

When the unchainèd soul awakens
From death's solemn sleep,
  Christ alone can calm her fears
  Through the eternal years.

Oh, then quickly seek thy Saviour,
Whilst He still is near!
  Time is hurrying fast away,
  Make no more delay.

At the Opening of a Convalescent Home.*

JESUS CHRIST, our true Physician,
　Prosper Thou our work to-day,
And Thy heavenly benediction
　Pour upon us as we pray ;
Bless all those who in Thy members
　Here shall minister to Thee,
Give them faith in every sufferer,
　Thee, their loving Lord, to see.

Bless, dear Lord, the souls that enter
　Here, Thy loving care to know ;
Let them taste the healing medicines
　Which from Thee for ever flow ;
Let them know the grace of pardon—
　Living faith and hope and love—
And so fit them, great Physician,
　For their heavenly home above.

---

* S. Elizabeth's House of Rest, Plympton S. Mary, July
28th, 1880, in memoriam Eliza Mary Middleton.

Bless all those who of their substance
　　Here shall offer gifts to Thee ;
Sevenfold into their bosoms
　　Give Thy mercy full and free.
Bless alike each humble sharer
　　In this sacred work of love,
That, when earthly toils are ended,
　　All may dwell with Thee above.

Friday Evening Hymn.

AGAIN night's shadows round us fall,
   The daylight dies away ;
My soul, thy evening sacrifice,
   To Christ thy Saviour pay.

Praise Him who on the painful Cross
   Reclined in death for thee,
That from the pains of endless death
   Thy soul He might set free.

O Jesu ! ill can we express
   The thanks our souls that thrill
For Thy unutterable love,
   Shown forth on Calvary's hill.

Yet Thou, O Lord, wilt not disdain
   The grateful, loving lays,
Which day and night we offer up
   To Thy eternal praise.

Thy Cross is on our brow, dear Lord ;
Oh, fix it deep within,
That we may prove its saving power
In crucifying sin!

Lord, may we now and ever rest
Securely in Thy love,
Till, all earth's gloomy shadows past,
We find true rest above.

To God the Father, God the Son,
And God the Spirit blest,
By men and angels evermore
Let praises be addressed.

Children's Hymns.

THE CHRISTIAN CHILD'S REPLY.

"Suffer little children to come unto Me."—*S. Matt.* xix. 14.

MERCIFUL and loving Saviour,
 God of heaven, and earth, and sea,
King of all the glorious angels,
 Dost Thou call me unto Thee?

I am poor, and weak, and sinful,
 Can I, Lord, be dear to Thee?
Yes; the blessed words are written,
 "Little children, come to Me."

Therefore, in my childhood's weakness,
 In my ignorance and sin,
I will come to Thee, dear Jesus,
 That Thy blessing I may win.

Fold me in Thy arms, and bless me,
    Even as Thou didst of old
Bless the children who drew near Thee,
    Thy sweet presence to behold.

Let Thy blessing rest upon me
    During all my earthly days,
Helping me to serve Thee truly,
    And to walk in Thy blest ways.

Glory be to Thee, Lord Jesus,
    Who wast once a Child for me ;
Grant me, Lord, at last to see Thee
    In Thy glorious majesty.

ROYAL CHILDREN.

WE are the children of a King
  Who reigns in heaven above,
Yet loves His children here below
  With true and perfect love ;
Who wills that we should live with Him,
  When this short life is o'er,
In his bright home of happiness
  And glory evermore.

To reach this bright and happy home
  We must our souls prepare,
For nothing sinful or impure
  Can ever enter there.
We must not shrink from serving Christ,
  Whate'er the world may say,
For Christ will never own the child
  Who turns from Him away.

As soldiers of our heavenly King,
　We must with courage fight;
Although we see Him not, we are
　For ever in His sight;
And earnestly He watches us,
　All through each day and night,
To see if we are true and brave
　Throughout our life-long fight.

Oh, children of the heavenly King,
　Remember this alway :
Christ promises to give us strength
　According to our day;
He will not leave us to ourselves
　In danger's trying hour,
But come to aid us in our need
　With heavenly strength and power.

Then let us fight the fight of faith,
　Since Jesus Christ is near;
With such a Captain for our Guide,
　What can we have to fear?

But let us always watch and pray,
  For such is Christ's command;
Then will He bring us home at last
  To heaven, our promised land.

Ah ! if we reach that blessèd home,
  Sweet will it be to sing,
With angels and the blessèd saints,
  Hymns to our heavenly King;
For ever and for evermore
  To join the heavenly host
In praising God the Father, Son,
  And God the Holy Ghost. Amen.

"*FOLLOW ME.*"

My Saviour has called me to follow Him on
To the bright home of glory to which He has gone.
Oh, shall I refuse Him, and cling to this earth,
And so miss the prize of my heavenly birth?

Many foes are around me ; ah ! this I know well ;
But Jesus has given me a heavenly spell :
'Tis to whisper His Name in the deep of my heart,
And then my soul's enemies quickly depart.

'Tis to make the dread sign which His enemies fear,
Which bad angels shrink from, and good ones draw near,
The sign of salvation, the life-giving Cross,
In which whoso glories can ne'er suffer loss.

Oh, then my soul's Captain looks down on the strife,
And bids me fight bravely for heaven and life !
He seems to say, " Courage ! Remember My love,
And think on the joys which await thee above."

Lord Jesus, I follow ; I will not say nay ;
But help me, dear Saviour, to keep the right way,
To suffer with patience all sorrow and loss,
And never prove faithless to Thee or Thy Cross.

And then, though the end of my struggle be near,
If Thou, Lord, art with me, oh ! what need I fear ?
My soul will be Thine as I draw my last breath,
And be guarded by Thee through the valley of death.

Oh, joy beyond thought, to be led safely on
To that blissful home where my Saviour has gone ;
To see Him, and hear Him, and know I am His,
For ever and ever in infinite bliss.

All this joy may be mine if, obeying His word,
I die daily to sin and follow my Lord ;
If I take up the cross which my Saviour now gives,
I shall dwell in the land where my Saviour now lives.

MORNING HYMN FOR CHILDREN.

Thy glory fills the heavens,
O King of boundless might !
The blessèd angels praise Thee there,
All clad in robes of white.

Thy glory fills the earth;
The sun, the stars, the sky,
All speak of the eternal King,
Who lives and rules on high.

Thy glory fills the Church,
Jesus came forth from Thee,
To purchase Her with His own Blood,
For ever Thine to be.

Yet dost Thou deign, O Lord,
Midst all this glory given,
To let our infant voices reach
Thee on Thy throne in heaven.

Oh, make us love Thee well,
Thou glorious One yet Three !
As long as life on earth shall last,
And through eternity.

EVENING HYMN FOR CHILDREN.

The day, O Lord, is Thine,
Thine also is the night,
Darkness and light to Thee are one,
Who art Thyself the Light.

Lord, we are also Thine;
We worship Thee alone;
For Thou didst at the holy fount
Adopt us for Thine own.

As children of the Light,
Oh, may we pure remain,
And never soil our garment bright
With aught of sinful stain.

O Guardian of our souls,
Who only hast the power,
Do Thou preserve our souls from sin
In dark temptation's hour.

To us, Thy children dear,
O Lord, Thine ear incline,
And whether it be night or day
Keep us for ever Thine.

Thine through life's toilsome way,
Thine when death draweth nigh,
Thine in the dreadful judgment-day,
Thine in eternity.

MISCELLANEOUS PIECES.

Silent Warnings.

SILENTLY, as shadows fall
   O'er the landscape bright,
Warning wandering travellers
   Of impending night,
Fall God's warnings on our souls,
   Throwing into shade
Visions fair of earthly bliss,
   Which our hearts have made.

Silently and solemnly
   Speaks God's voice within,
Telling us of wasted days
   Stained with many a sin,

o

Bidding us God's mercy seek
In the day of grace,
Lest we miss one vision bright—
God's all-pardoning face.

Silently, as breaks the sun
' Through the morning haze,
Driving far the shades of night
With its conquering rays,
Works the mighty grace of God
Our dark souls within,
Conquering satanic craft,
And the power of sin.

Silently, as days rush by,
Sinking into past,
Leading to one day on earth
Which must be our last,
So our thoughts and words and acts
Stamp our souls for aye,
For a home of endless night,
Or of endless day.

The Soul's Lament.

"Jesus, I cannot love Thee!
  This is my deepest grief;
And for this sorrow Thou, Lord,
  Alone canst give relief.
Oh, light again the embers
  Of that pure fire divine,
Which purifies the spirit,
  And makes it wholly Thine!

"Jesus, I cannot love Thee!
  Yet, dear Lord, tell me why
The fount of my affections
  Is now so parched and dry?
Have chains of sinful habit,
  Stretching through my life past,
Exhausted Thy long-suffering,
  And wearied Thee at last?

"Jesus, I cannot love Thee!
Is there some secret sin
Lurking within my spirit,
    Stopping Thine entrance in?
Or is some earthly idol
    Enthroned within my heart,
From which, e'en for Thy love, Lord,
    I cannot wholly part?

"Jesus, I cannot love Thee!
    My heart must bear the pain
Of utter desolation
    Until I love again.
O Lord, dispel the darkness;
    Send sunshine through the gloom
Which shrouds around my spirit—
    The darkness of the tomb.

"Jesus, I cannot love Thee!
    And yet, to win my love,
Thou camest, Lord, in mercy,
    From highest heaven above,

To bear all shame and sorrow,
　　Abandonment and loss,
And die a death of anguish
　　Upon the shameful Cross."

Thus spake I in my spirit
　　To Jesus Christ, my Lord,
Because my heart seemed frozen
　　Towards Him whom I adored.
Nature appeared o'erclouded,
　　Nothing was bright to see,
Because my loving Saviour
　　Had hid His face from me.

But, hark ! I hear a new voice,
　　Moving my soul within ;
'Tis like the breath of morning
　　Across a sultry plain ;
'Tis like melodious music
　　Breaking upon mine ear ;
It kindles faith and hope and love,
　　And drives away my fear.

It is the voice of Jesus,
　Thus o'er my spirit shed,
Kindling life's smoking embers
　When they were almost dead ;
Speaking of love unchanging,
　Even for such as me ;
Drawing my gaze upon Him,
　That I His love might see.

"Art thou in desolation?
　Child of my love," said He,
"And sad and sorrowful, because
　Thou feel'st no love for Me ?
Give Me thy grief and sorrow,
　It shows me thou art true,
In spite of the sore burden
　Which so oppresses you.

"But, oh, remember ever,
　Those who with Me would reign
Must not shrink back from sorrow,
　Or weariness, or pain.

Gethsemane was dark to Me,
And darker still that space
When on the Cross, my Father
Appeared to hide His face.

"Thou canst not love Me deeply,
This is thy sorrow true;
Love is not what thou feelest
Is to thy Saviour due;
Yet give what thou canst give Me,
Thy grief I count as part,
And take it as the offering
Of thy whole will and heart."

Oh hear how full and princely
Is my Redeemer's love;
Deeper than depths of ocean,
Higher than heaven above;
Wider than east from west is,
And stronger far than death,—
Lord Jesus, I will love Thee,
E'en to my latest breath.

The Great Physician.

"Is there no balm in Gilead; is there no physician there?"
Jer. viii. 22.

OH ! is there no Balsam in Gilead's fair country?
No balm the keen anguish of souls to relieve?
No skilful physician to pity our sorrows,
And all the deep pains of our souls to relieve?

All weary and heart-broken, sin-stained and sorrowful,
No human physician can soothe our deep pain;
But one great Physician has come down from heaven,
Who knows how to heal wounded spirits again.

One Balsam alone can remove our soul's sickness,
Cure all our diseases and soothe all our pain;
One Balm has the virtue to calm all our troubles,
And give us back health, joy, and comfort again.

That Balm issues forth from the tree on the mountain
On which the great price of redemption was paid,
Where Jesus our Saviour, to win our salvation,
A full satisfaction for all our sins made.

Behold the true Balm pouring forth from the Victim,
    To heal all the nations who trust in its might;
The soul which it touches is cured of its sickness,
    And stands pure and healthy in God's holy sight.

Lord Jesus, Thou art this Almighty Physician,
    And Gilead's choice Balm is Thy own precious
        Blood;
It flows from Thy five wounds, as from a deep fountain,
    To heal contrite souls in its life-giving flood.

I come to Thee, Jesus, my soul's true Physician,
    To tell all my sorrows, my sin, and my grief,
Yet trusting Thy mercy, Thy love, and Thy power,
    To grant me free pardon and blissful relief.

For now, as of old, from the tree on the mountain
    Streams forth the red Balm in its virtue divine;
Souls countless have found in it health and salvation;
    Lord Jesus, apply this sweet Balsam to mine.

Oh, then with new zeal shall I sing forth Thy praises,
    And love Thee as one who has had much forgiven,
Until, ever kept by Thy grace and Thy power,
    I finish my journey and praise Thee in heaven!

The Storm of Life.

"Without were fightings, within were fears."—2 *Cor.* vii. 5.

THE storm of life around my soul
   Is raging in its might;
Black are the clouds, and lowering;
   I see no gleam of light.
Daily my sad companions are
   Sorrow, and pain, and grief;
Merciful Saviour, visit me,
   And bring my soul relief.

As Thou, my Lord, of old didst walk
   Upon the stormy wave,
When Thy disciples struggled hard
   Their beaten ship to save,
So let me see Thy form, dear Lord,
   In love approaching me,
As I my weary strife maintain
   On life's tempestuous sea.

Let me not sink, my gracious Lord,
  Beneath temptation's power;
Stretch forth Thine hand, and hold me up
  In this my soul's dark hour.
My only trust for safety lies
  In Thy almighty aid;
Oh, say then to my sinking soul,
  "'Tis I, be not afraid!"

Desolation and Consolation.

DESOLATION.

CLOUDED is the day, and dreary;
Light and comfort all are gone;
I must tread life's painful journey
Sad and weary, and alone.

Earthly joys have all departed,
Heavenly joys I cannot taste;
Storms have passed across my spirit,
All is desolate and waste.

CONSOLATION.

"Look up, sinful, but beloved one!
Seest thou not upon the wild,
One whose look is that of pity,
For His own, though erring, child?

" Is there nothing that can win thee
In that sweet reproving glance?
Nothing that can melt thy spirit,
And thy very soul entrance?

" Hast thou not some love to give Him,
Who His life-blood gave for thee?
Hast thou not an end for living,
When He calls thee His to be?

" To the wilderness He calls thee,
Not to pine in useless grief,
But that He may be thy portion,
Rest and joy, and sweet relief."

FAITH AND LOVE REKINDLED.

Patient, gentle, loving Saviour,
Canst Thou wish me to be Thine?
Open wide my heart, and fill it;
Be Thou altogether mine.

Nerve my soul, dear Lord, for action;
Teach me how to serve Thee best;
" All for Jesus," be my watchword,
Till I gain my heavenly rest.

Too late!

"Now is the accepted time."—2 *Cor.* vi. 2.
"Strive to enter in at the strait gate: for many, I say unto you,
will seek to enter in, and shall not be able."

S. Luke xiii. 24.

Too late! too late! ye cannot enter now;
Closed is the door; thy day of grace is past;
The loving patience thou didst madly spurn
All through thy life, exhausted is at last.

The door of mercy once was open wide;
In loving accents Jesus called thee in,
To share, with all His saints, His rich repast:
Thou didst prefer to feed on husks of sin,

Out in the darkness of eternal night,
Banished for ever from thy Saviour's face,
Must thou endure the wages thou hast earned—
Remorse and endless pain, shame and disgrace.

"Jesu, my Saviour, save me from this doom;
Save me, my Lord, in spite of all my sin :
I hear Thy voice; the door is not yet closed;
Through Thy unbounded love, oh, let me in !

"Too long, too long, my Lord, have earthly joys
And sinful pleasures held my soul in thrall;
But now I hear Thy voice, and come to Thee,
Seeking for grace to crucify them all.

"Jesu, Thy Name is Saviour ! Thou hast said,
Those who seek Thee Thou wilt not cast away :
I seek Thee, Lord; I long to know Thy will,
That I may do it better every day.

"Yet help me, Jesus, by Thy mighty grace,
Never again to tread the ways of sin ;
Never again to spurn Thy loving calls ;
But in my day pardon and peace to win.

"By faith I see Thee, Lord, upon the Cross,
Bleeding to death in untold agony ;
It was for sinners that Thou thus didst die ;
And if for sinners, then, O Lord, for me.

" Therefore I fly to Thee in my soul's need.
  Oh, let me share Thy mercy full and free !
  Say to my soul, ' "Tis still thy day of grace ;
  I died for all men, and I died for thee.'

" And ere Thou givest me my final call,
  Oh, wash my soul from every stain of sin
  In the all-cleansing Fountain of Thy Blood !
  Then open heaven's gate, and let me in."

209

Loneliness.

ALONE, alone in the wide, wide world!
  Alone, and well-nigh broken-hearted,
I lived and I laboured for those I loved,
  And from those I must now be parted.

Alone, alone in the wide, wide world!
  Misjudged, malignèd, and forsaken;
Few are the ties which bind me to earth,
  And these from me soon will be taken.

Alone, alone in the wide, wide world!
  Day and night my poor spirit is aching,
As slowly earth's idols sink down in the dust,
  And my soul to the truth is awaking.

Alone, alone in the wide, wide world!
  Yet my heart for affection is bursting,
As the parchèd sand, in the desert wild,
  For the showers of heaven is thirsting.

P

Oh, no ! not alone in the wide, wide world,
    Forget not, O soul, thy vocation ;
There is ONE at least who offers thee love,
    In this thy sad time of probation.

'Tis the Shepherd true of the wandering one,
    Who is watching thy soul's desolation ;
And tenderly waiting, with loving care,
    For the moment to give consolation.

That moment will be when thy heart is weaned
    From seeking an earthly treasure,
Or mourning over thy broken reeds
    With feelings beyond due measure ;

When sorrow has taught thee the lesson true—
    That nothing in all creation
Can satisfy fully the heart of man,
    Save Jesus and His salvation.

No longer alone in the wide, wide world,
    If He is thy Friend and Brother ;
Then canst thou endure all its sorrows and toils,
    For rest and true joy in another.

Home.

HOME, home, home!
Who does not long for home?
  Though we may stray
  Far, far away,
We ever long for home.

Home, home, home!
Vision of peace, sweet home!
  Midst toil and strife
  Of daily life,
Our dream of rest is home.

Home, home, home!
Our childhood's happy home!
  O vision bright
  Of joy and light,
Our dear departed home.

Home, home, home!
Our future happy home!
  Oh, guide us right,
  Thou one true Light,
To our eternal home!

The Loving Calls of Jesus.

I HEARD the voice of Jesus,
Early in life's long day,
Ere yet the dreams of childhood
Had wholly passed away.
Kneeling beside my mother,
Or on my father's knee,
That sweet voice seemed to utter,
"Dear child, come unto Me."

And through that dreamy period
When everything was new,
And all new things looked pleasant,
And beautiful and true,
There seemed a want within me
Which nought around could fill ;
It was the voice of Jesus,
Calling me to Him still.

I heard the voice of Jesus,
   As sped youth's golden hours,
When life seemed bathed in sunshine,
   And earth a land of flowers.
A sudden yet sweet sadness
   Oft held my heart in thrall,
And Jesus seemed to whisper,
   " Dear child, this is not all;

These joys are short and fleeting;
   These pleasures stored with pain;
For oft upon thy spirit
   They leave a guilty stain.
Give not thy best affections
   To these poor things of earth;
But on thy rightful country,
   Child of a heavenly birth.

I heard the voice of Jesus,
   When youth had passed away;
It sounded sad and graver
   Than in my childhood's day.

It spake of calls neglected,
Of sinful actions done;
Of Christian gifts and graces
Which I had never won.

" Oh, why didst thou not listen
To all my accents mild,
And seek and find Me early,
Beloved, but erring child?
Why didst thou shun thy Saviour,
When in sweet words of love
I called thee from earth's trifles
To the true joys above?"

Thus spake the voice of Jesus;
It filled my soul with fears,
Until, with contrite spirit,
And penitential tears,
I laid all bare before Him
My life so stained and wild,
And prayed Him still to pity
His wayward, sinful child.

But what is that dread vision
On which He bids me gaze?

Himself upon a Cross raised,
　Dying in agonies;
His head and hands, His feet and side,
　Are pierced and wounded sore;
His pure and spotless body
　Covered with bloody gore.

'Twas all, 'twas all to save thee,"
　His voice now seemed to say,
"That I endured to die thus
　In untold agony.
To win for thee salvation
　I poured forth all My Blood:
Draw near, and wash thy spirit
　In this all-cleansing flood."

I heard the voice of Jesus;
　It pierced my inmost soul;
I answered, "Lord, I give Thee
　My heart, my life, my all.
Freely for me, dear Saviour,
　Thy Blood has been outpoured;
Oh, freely let me give back
　Love to Thee, dearest Lord!"

Offerings.

" What shall I render unto the Lord for all His benefits towards me?"—*Psalm* cxvi. 12.

WHAT offering shall I bring my Lord,
　Before His altar bending ;
Who died for me upon the Cross,
　To win me life unending?
Jesu, what can I offer Thee
Who didst Thy life-blood give for me?

I look within, but nought I see
　Which I can dare to proffer ;
Some sighs, and tears, and broken vows,
　Are all I have to offer.
Alas ! my Lord, I am not meet
To kneel before Thy mercy-seat.

Yet for poor sinners, Lord, Thou art
   Still with Thy Church abiding,
As God and man 'neath earthly veils
   Thy glorious presence hiding.
'Tis Thy delight still to reside
With those for whose sake Thou hast died.

Therefore I come to worship Thee
   With loving adoration,
To plead anew Thy sacrifice
   For my entire salvation.
Thee, Jesus, God and man, to own
Upon Thy lowly altar throne.

The Reed in the Wilderness.

"What went ye out for to see? A reed shaken with the
wind?"—*S. Matt.* xi. 7.

LIGHTLY play the summer breezes
O'er the sandy desert wild;
Lightly bends the reed so graceful
Yielding to the zephyr mild.

Lightly round man's fragile spirit
Plays temptation's subtle power;
Lightly man yields to its breathings
Every day and every hour.

Fiercely howls the gushing tempest,
Wildly flies the blinding sand;
Strongest reeds lie bruised and broken
On the torn and wasted land.

Fiercely blow the storms of passion
Round man's soul with scorching breath;
Oft he bends and breaks before them,
Lying bound in sin and death.

Meekly doth our loving Saviour
   Hold the reed in His right Hand—
Symbol of His saintly power
   O'er the foes who round Him stand.

Thus the symbol of man's weakness—
   A reed shaken by the wind—
Is now made a sign of power
   By our Saviour true and kind.

Though, like reeds, we may be shaken;
   Yet, if held in Jesus' hand,
We may overcome temptation,
   And before our foes may stand.

Stand, because upheld by Jesus
   In the strength by Jesus given;
Till, our stormy trials ended,
   We shall reign with Him in heaven.

Then the reed once weak and feeble,
   Raised again from earthly sod,
Shall be fixed a stedfast pillar
   In the temple of our God.

Jesus Reigning from the Tree.

Lord Jesus Christ, true God and man,
How vast that love, and free,
Which drew Thee down from heaven's high throne
To reign from off the Tree!

All things proclaim Thy boundless love—
The heaven, the earth, the sea;
Yet man the lesson chiefly learns
Beneath the plain Cross Tree.

Thy presence fills the universe,
And floods all heaven with bliss;
Yet is it fixed on every soul,
In such a world as this;

For, lifted on the Cross, my Lord,
Thou speakest thus to me:
"O Christian soul, remember well
I suffered thus for thee—

" To save thy soul from endless loss,
  And untold misery;
And win for thee a place in heaven
  With all My own and ME.

" Oh, look on ME, and be ye saved!
  Sinners, to ME draw nigh!
Rob ME not of the longed-for fruit
  Of all My agony!

" The thorny crown upon My brow
  Is but the kingly sign
Of love to reign in human hearts,
  And make them wholly Mine.

" Mine, as they tread life's thorny way;
  Mine, when they come to die;
Mine, in the awful judgment-day;
  Mine, in eternity."

Lord Jesus Christ, my God and King,
  Who can resist the grace
Of that deep love and tenderness
  Which beameth from Thy face?

Like needle to the loadstone drawn,
By strong magnetic might,
So souls that gaze on Thee, dear Lord,
Cling to the wondrous sight,

Until that vision fills their souls
With that all-cleansing love
Which purifies, and makes them meet
For love's true home above.

The Symbol of the Cross.

WHENE'ER the figure of the Cross
  With loving faith I view,
It speaks with silent eloquence
  Of many a symbol true.

'Tis like the key of Paradise,
  Without which man must be
Shut out from his own blessèd home
  Throughout eternity.

To feeble souls 'tis like a staff
  Which guides them on their way,
Through all this world's ensnaring paths
  To heaven's eternal day.

To penitents 'tis like a star
  Which shines with radiance bright,
And draws them with a loving power
  To Christ, the one true Light.

To faithful souls 'tis like a shield
　　Which guards them from their foes,
And gives them in their sharpest strife
　　Courage and calm repose.

To those whom Satan tempts to sin
　　In life's long deadly fight,
'Tis like a sword which cuts his power
　　With Christ's all-conquering might.

'Tis like a ladder fixed on earth,
　　Yet reaching far away,
Leading all those who mount thereon
　　To realms of endless day.

It is the symbol of Christ's love
　　Even for such as me.
Oh, may its vision, dearest Lord,
　　Fix my whole heart on Thee !

The Church's Morning Call.

AGAIN the call to early prayer
  Sounds through the dewy morning,
Inviting us, in God's own house,
  To seek our souls' adorning.
O Lord, do thou our hearts prepare
To find Thy gracious presence there.

Let not dull sloth, oppressing us,
  Our souls from Thee e'er sever;
But rouse our slumbering faculties
  To love and serve Thee ever;
That so each passing day may be
A step which brings us nearer Thee.

To earth's absorbing vanities
  May we ne'er homage render,
Or have our souls in bondage held
  By earthly pomp or splendour;
But in Thy footsteps, gracious Lord,
Press onward to our high reward.

The Words of Jesus.

" How sweet are Thy words unto my taste !"—*Psalm* cxix. 103.

SWEET are the words of Jesus,
    As through life's toilsome road
We tread our weary journey
    To Zion's blest abode.

Sweet are the words of Jesus,
    When, compassed round with sin,
We seek some living power
    To strengthen us within.

Sweet are the words of Jesus,
    When best loved friends are gone,
And we must tread life's journey
    More sadly and alone.

Sweet are the words of Jesus,
    When, on the bed of pain,
The cup our Father gives us
    In loving trust we drain.

Sweet are the words of Jesus,
 When death is drawing nigh,
And all life's scenes and actions
 Like dreams are passing by.

But, oh ! how sweet Thy words, Lord,
 When, on the eternal shore,
We hear Thee bid us welcome
 To life for evermore.

O Jesu, loving Saviour,
 Make all this sweetness mine !
Wean me from all earth's idols,
 And make me wholly Thine.

The Lost Piece Found.

'Tis found, tis found at last,
My missing coin is found ;
Twas buried amidst earthly things
Which compassed it around.

I sought it carefully,
Carefully and with tears ;
I thought it was for ever lost ;
My heart was filled with fears.

But Jesus knew my pain,
And Jesus knew my fears,
And Jesus shewed me where to look,
And wiped away my tears.

Tis found, tis found ! O joy,
Eternal life is mine,
If I but keep the precious prize
In my soul's inmost shrine.

A Still Small Voice.

I HEAR my Saviour's voice
   Speaking my soul within,
Bidding me seek His pardoning grace,
   And shun the ways of sin.

I hear my Saviour's voice
   Bidding me bring my grief,
My pains, my sorrows, and my cares,
   To Him for sweet relief.

I hear my Saviour's voice
   Bidding me bear my cross,
In faith and meekness after Him,
   Counting all else as loss.

I hear my Saviour's voice
   Speaking in deepest love,
Bidding me shun earth's empty joys
   And seek true joys above.

O Jesu ! through Thy grace
　I will Thy voice obey ;
And spurning the broad road of sin,
　Walk in the narrow way—

The narrow way of life,
　Which leads to heaven and Thee ;
To know Thee, love Thee, praise Thy name
　Throughout eternity.

Light in Darkness.

"Sorrow not as others who have no hope."—1 *Thess.* iv. 13.

My sweet child is gone home
For evermore to rest,
Free from all sin and pain,
Safe on his Saviour's breast,
Amidst the angels bright,
And ransomed spirits blest.

My sweet child is gone home,
His soul has found release
From earthly toils and cares,
And reached a land of peace,
Where pain can never come,
Where tears for ever cease.

My sweet child is gone home
To taste that heavenly joy,
Free from all taint of sin,
Pure, and without alloy,
Which, throughout endless day,
Can never, never cloy.

My sweet child is gone home ;
Jesus, Thou wert his guide
Through life's brief trial-time,
And through dark Jordan's tide,
Until he reached his home,
Thy wounded, sheltering side.

My sweet child is gone home ;
Oh, how I love to say,
Again and yet again,
Throughout the weary day,
" My sweet child is gone home
To dwell with Christ alway !"

Lord, not again on earth
Can I my loved child see ;
But bring me to that home
Where now he dwells with Thee,
There to rest in Thy love
Throughout eternity.

The Child's Heavenly Vision.*

IN MEMORIAM K. E. W.

WHAT dost thou see, fair child? Rapt is thy gaze
On some bright vision which we cannot see.
Is it an angel sent to guide thy steps
Through suffering to a blest eternity?
Or is thy Saviour speaking to thy soul
In loving accents thou alone canst hear,
Calling thee to Himself with fondling smile,
Kindling thy love and soothing all thy fear?

---

* On looking at the portrait of my grandchild, Kenred
Eardley Wilmot, who died at three years of age, painted at
Florence by my son Edward, November, 1878. The picture
represents a child turning away from his toys to grasp at a
butterfly—emblem of the resurrection. His attention seems
drawn aside from the butterfly to something which he alone
sees beyond—a messenger from heaven calling him home.

The toys of earth have now no charm for thee,
For heaven's joys are breaking on thy sight.
The painted butterfly may flutter by,
But it checks not thy spirit's upward flight
Towards brighter scenes in blissful Paradise,
Where God sheds all around perpetual day,
And in the streets of New Jerusalem
The boys and girls in heavenly transport play.*

Oh, blissful lot ! to go in childhood's days
To meet thy Saviour, without shame or sin,
Untainted with the world's defiling ways,
To bud and blossom Paradise within,
And learn the blessed alphabet of heaven,
How best thy God and Saviour to adore,
How best to join in those sweet hymns of praise
Which saints and angels sing for evermore.

S. Michael and All Angels,
    S. PETER'S, 1879.

---

* "And the streets of the city shall be full of boys and girls playing in the streets thereof."—*Zech.* viii. 5.

In Memoriam

CHARLES FUGE LOWDER, M.A.,
Vicar of S. Peter's, London Docks, E.

Qu. ob. Sept. 9th, 1880, in the Austrian Tyrol.

"MORS JANUA VITÆ."

THE standard-bearers of the Lord
   Are falling one by one;
Calmly they die within their ranks
   When their Lord's work is done—
They pass from suffering, toil, and strife,
To rest and everlasting life.

And as they pass behind the veil
   Which hides them from our sight,
They meet their Saviour's loving face,
   And know that rest, and light,
And blissful hope beyond all price,
Which souls enjoy in Paradise.

Though dead, they speak to us, and say,
    "Stand firm ; be true, and brave ;
Trust in your Lord when foes press on,
    For He is strong to save ;
And if you fall in His great fight,
Fear not ; death is the gate of life."

"Lord, give us grace to follow them
    As they have followed Thee,
That where Thy faithful servants are
    There we may also be,
And live and reign with them and Thee
Throughout a blest eternity.

A Little While.

"Thy people have possessed it but for a little while."
Isa. lxiii. 18.

A LITTLE while, a little while,
  And this short life will seem
As unsubstantial as the thoughts
  Which haunt us in a dream.

A little while of pain and grief,
  Of suffering, shame, and loss ;
A little while to strive with sin,
  And bear our Saviour's cross.

A little while of faithful work,
  Filled with a Saviour's love,
Then a long while of happiness
  With our dear Lord above.

The Shadows of Evening.

THE shadows of evening are falling around us,
The day and its duties are passing away ;
Oh come, and ere night in deep slumber has bound us,
Recall one by one the events of the day.

Think well on the motives that prompted each action,
Think well on the thoughts that gave birth to each word;
Oh, see if aught sinful in will or affection
Has raised up a shadow 'twixt thee and thy Lord !

And ere thou committest thy soul to His keeping,
Who all the day long has been close at thy side,
Bewail every sin which can trouble thy sleeping,
Then calmly thy soul to His mercy confide.

And when in deep slumber thy powers forsake thee,
His arms everlasting are under thee still,
His ministering angels are watching around thee,
To guard and protect thee from every ill.

Thus calmly reposing in God's gracious keeping,
As souls rest in Paradise when life is o'er,
Fresh strength to serve Him shall He grant to thy
  sleeping,
Until thy last sleep makes thee His evermore.

Light at Evening Time.

" It shall come to pass, that at evening time there shall be light."
Zech. xiv. 7.

" THERE shall be light at evening time ; "
  Oh, let this light be mine, dear Lord,
  According to Thy gracious word !
  For clouds are gathering round my way
  Which speak of nature's closing day,
  And nought can dissipate the gloom
  Which hovers round the darksome tomb,
  Save light from Thee at evening time.

Passing Away.

PASSING away, passing away,
The visions of life are passing away :
As a dream that flies at the opening day,
The visions of life are passing away.

Lasting for aye, lasting for aye,
Our thoughts, words, and actions are lasting for aye ;
They will meet us again at the last great day,
Though now they all seem to be passing away !

Submission.

I WILL lie still, my God; I will lie still,
Whilst Thou dost work in me Thy holy will;
I will not shrink, or murmur, or repine,
If Thou wilt strengthen me, and keep me Thine.

I know, my God, that all who heaven would win,
Pain must endure—the penalty of sin;
Yet suffering, by Thy grace, is made to be
A means of fitting us for heaven and Thee.

Frail nature shrinks, and fain would heaven gain
Without Thy needful discipline of pain;
Therefore on Thee alone I will depend
To keep me calm and patient to the end.

Q 2

Submission.

And when death draweth nigh, O Lord, be near,
To keep me faithful and subdue my fear,
To drive away sin and Satanic power,
Lest they assail my soul in that dread hour.

And when I breathe frail nature's latest sigh,
Then, Jesus—Light and Life—be very nigh ;
And, by Thy all-prevailing sacrifice,
Grant me an entrance into Paradise.

DOMESTIC PIECES.

DOMESTIC PIECES.

The Town Girl's First Visit to the Country.

LITTLE EMILY AND THE SPOTTY PIG.

THERE was a little spotty pig,
    Who was so fond of play ;
He teased his mammy all the night,
    And grunted all the day.

One day as on the meadow green
    He trotted all about,
He saw, just at the garden gate,
    A little girl come out.

Now when this naughty little pig
    The little girl did spy,
He said, " I 'll trot and grunt until
    I make this town girl cry."

So up he trots to Emily,
    Squeaking, and dancing jigs,

R

Till she runs crying in, and says,
"Ma, I don't like the pigs!"

Swift to the rescue runs Papa,
And says, "You naughty pigs,
How dare you tease my little girl
With squeaky grunts and jigs!"

Young piggy squeaked, and ran away;
Pa looked so black and big;
"I'm sure," thought Spotty to himself,
"He could eat up a pig.

"But I'll have out my fun," he said,
"Upon another day;
And trot and grunt at Emily,
When Pappy's gone away."

I do not know whether or not
Young Spotty kept his plan;
But if he did, when Pa comes back   ·
He'll catch him if he can,

And pull his little curly tail
Until he squeaks outright,
For putting little Emily
In such a dreadful fright.

HORRABRIDGE, *June,* 1866.

"Are there any Spotty Pigs there?"

MESSAGE FROM EMILY.

My darling Emily,
> Whene'er I take my walks abroad,
> No spotty pigs I see;
> But all around, where'er I look,
> 'Tis rock, and sky, and sea.

> And yet outside our window low
> There are some creatures too,
> Who every morning wake Papa
> With "Cock-a-doodle-doo."

> There is a very large black cock,
> Another red and blue,
> And several little ones; but all
> Cry, "Cock-a-doodle-doo!"

> I cannot think what they can mean;
> Dear Emily, can you?
> They might as well say, "Nussing, Pa," *
> As, "Cock-a-doodle-doo."

* Emily's favourite reply.

"Oh, dear, good, pretty little cocks,
  Don't make such a to-do ;
Stop a few minutes from your song
  Of 'Cock-a-doodle-doo.'

"You will not stop?   Then really I
  Must wish you all adieu ;"
The only answer that I got
  Was, "Cock-a-doodle-doo."

All send their love to you, dear pet ;
  I shall be back quite soon ;
You may look out for me, I think,
  On Wednesday afternoon.

                    Your very loving

                              PAPPY.

BOSCASTLE, *June*, 1868.

Donkey-land.

My darling Gerty,—

Not far from here, the people said,
  There was a lovely beach ;
And, if we could a carriage get,
  'Twas not beyond our reach.

We got a carriage, and set out,
  The children full of glee ;
Papa in front, Mamma behind,
  With children one, two, three.

And didn't all enjoy the drive,
  Round by Tintagel bold ;
And didn't the stern castle
  Look beautiful and old.

We wandered midst the rugged paths,
  We thought on days gone by,
Now hidden by time's hoary veil
  In shroud of mystery ;

Of gallant knights, now laid in dust,
    Who once, at Arthur's call,
Had issued forth to win high fame
    Through yonder archèd wall.

The storms of many centuries,
    Charged with Atlantic blasts,
Had beat against these crumbling stones,
    Yet still the ruin lasts—

Still speaks, with silent voice, of times
    Which we no more may see,
When men lived not for self and gold,
    But deeds of chivalry.

We drove on by the sounding sea,
    Between two points of land ;
And then we all got out, to run
    Upon the yellow sand.

But first we called on Jenny Brown,
    Who lives close by the shore,
And may have done, for aught I know,
    For twenty years or more.

Her great vocation in this life,
  As far as one can see,
Is to watch donkeys carrying sand,
  Boil water, and make tea.

Some small investments here we made,
  And in our baskets laid,
Consisting of tough-cakes and buns,
  Sweetstuff and lemonade.

Then we sat down upon a rock
  (There was no chair or stool);
'Twas very pleasant:—" Mammy dear,
  Your dress is in the pool !"

Then each one took a pasty, and
  Each one began to eat,
When, all at once, we found the sea
  Was all around our feet.

" Oh ! oh ! oh ! oh !" cried Mammy dear;
  " Oh ! oh !" cried children three;
" You need not fear at all," said Pa,
  " You 're safe here from the sea;

" The tide is really going out,
  Although it looks so rough :
Lu, will you have more pasty, dear,
  Or lemonady stuff?"

A long row of brown donkeys now
  Came down upon the shore ;
There must have been full twenty-five,
  I think, or even more.

We watched them as they walked about
  Upon Trebarwith sand,
And said, " Henceforth the name must be
  Changed into ' Donkey-land.'"

Then, after many pleasant hours
  Spent by the foaming sea,
We all returned to Boscastle,
  As happy as could be.

                              Your loving

                                    PAPPY.

BOSCASTLE, *June*, 1868.

Our Moorland Home.

WE 'RE off to our moorland home,
Now summer's bright days have come;
    We don't much grieve
    The old town to leave,
O'er valley and tor to roam.

And we 'll scamper across the heather,
With hearts as light as a feather;
    From morning to night
    'Twill be our delight,
To be out in the balmy weather.

And we 'll wander amongst the trees,
And be fanned by the moorland breeze,
    And read nice books,
    In sweet little nooks,
Where nobody hears or sees.

And the absent ones will come down
From college and dusty town ;
'Twill add to our joys
When our dear brother boys
Come all our delights to crown.

Then hey for our moorland home,
Now summer's bright days have come !
We don't much grieve
The dull town to leave,
O'er valley and tor to roam.

Tor Royal, *May,* 1870.

PLYMOUTH :
W. BRENDON AND SON, PRINTERS, GEORGE STREET.

www.ingramcontent.com/pod-product-compliance
Lightning Source LLC
Chambersburg PA
CBHW030638030726
47497CB00006B/1852